JOSHUA

THE IGNATIUS CATHOLIC STUDY BIBLE

REVISED STANDARD VERSION
SECOND CATHOLIC EDITION

JOSHUA

With Introduction, Commentary, and Notes

by

Scott Hahn and Curtis Mitch

with

Michael Barber

and

with Study Questions by

Dennis Walters

IGNATIUS PRESS SAN FRANCISCO

Original RSV Bible text:
Nihil Obstat: Thomas Hanlon, S.T.L., L.S.S., Ph.L.
Imprimatur: +Peter W. Bartholome, D.D.
Bishop of Saint Cloud, Minnesota
May 11, 1966

Introduction, commentaries and notes:
Nihil obstat: Dr. Ruth Ohm Sutherland, Ph.D., Censor Deputatis
Imprimatur: + The Most Reverend Salvatore Cordileone
Archbishop of San Francisco
August 12, 2016

The *nihil obstat* and *imprimatur* are official declarations that a book or pamphlet is free of doctrinal or moral error. No implication is contained therein that those who have granted the *nihil obstat* and *imprimatur* agree with the contents, opinions, or statements expressed.

Cover art:
Joshua urges on his army outside the walls of Jericho
Anonymous, 1860
Photograph: HIP/Art Resource, N.Y.

Cover design by Riz Boncan Marsella

Published by Ignatius Press in 2017

Introductions, commentaries, notes, headings, and study questions
© 2017 by Ignatius Press, San Francisco
All rights reserved
ISBN 978-1-58617-910-6
Printed in the United States of America ∞

CONTENTS

INTRODUCTION TO THE IGNATIUS STUDY BIBLE

by Scott Hahn, Ph.D.

You are approaching the "word of God". This is the title Christians most commonly give to the Bible, and the expression is rich in meaning. It is also the title given to the Second Person of the Blessed Trinity, God the Son. For Jesus Christ became flesh for our salvation, and "the name by which he is called is The Word of God" (Rev 19:13; cf. Jn 1:14).

The word of God is Scripture. The Word of God is Jesus. This close association between God's *written* word and his *eternal* Word is intentional and has been the custom of the Church since the first generation. "All Sacred Scripture is but one book, and this one book is Christ, 'because all divine Scripture speaks of Christ, and all divine Scripture is fulfilled in Christ' "[1] (CCC 134). This does not mean that the Scriptures are divine in the same way that Jesus is divine. They are, rather, divinely inspired and, as such, are unique in world literature, just as the Incarnation of the eternal Word is unique in human history.

Yet we can say that the inspired word resembles the incarnate Word in several important ways. Jesus Christ is the Word of God incarnate. In his humanity, he is like us in all things, except for sin. As a work of man, the Bible is like any other book, except without error. Both Christ and Scripture, says the Second Vatican Council, are given "for the sake of our salvation" (*Dei Verbum* 11), and both give us God's definitive revelation of himself. We cannot, therefore, conceive of one without the other: the Bible without Jesus, or Jesus without the Bible. Each is the interpretive key to the other. And because Christ is the subject of all the Scriptures, St. Jerome insists, "Ignorance of the Scriptures is ignorance of Christ"[2] (CCC 133).

When we approach the Bible, then, we approach Jesus, the Word of God; and in order to encounter Jesus, we must approach him in a prayerful study of the inspired word of God, the Sacred Scriptures.

Inspiration and Inerrancy The Catholic Church makes mighty claims for the Bible, and our acceptance of those claims is essential if we are to read the Scriptures and apply them to our lives as the Church intends. So it is not enough merely to nod at words like "inspired", "unique", or "inerrant". We

have to understand what the Church means by these terms, and we have to make that understanding our own. After all, what we believe about the Bible will inevitably influence the way we read the Bible. The way we read the Bible, in turn, will determine what we "get out" of its sacred pages.

These principles hold true no matter what we read: a news report, a search warrant, an advertisement, a paycheck, a doctor's prescription, an eviction notice. How (or whether) we read these things depends largely upon our preconceived notions about the reliability and authority of their sources—and the potential they have for affecting our lives. In some cases, to misunderstand a document's authority can lead to dire consequences. In others, it can keep us from enjoying rewards that are rightfully ours. In the case of the Bible, both the rewards and the consequences involved take on an ultimate value.

What does the Church mean, then, when she affirms the words of St. Paul: "All Scripture is inspired by God" (2 Tim 3:16)? Since the term "inspired" in this passage could be translated "God-breathed", it follows that God breathed forth his word in the Scriptures as you and I breathe forth air when we speak. This means that God is the primary author of the Bible. He certainly employed human authors in this task as well, but he did not merely assist them while they wrote or subsequently approve what they had written. God the Holy Spirit is the *principal* author of Scripture, while the human writers are *instrumental* authors. These human authors freely wrote everything, and only those things, that God wanted: the word of God in the very words of God. This miracle of dual authorship extends to the whole of Scripture, and to every one of its parts, so that whatever the human authors affirm, God likewise affirms through their words.

The principle of biblical inerrancy follows logically from this principle of divine authorship. After all, God cannot lie, and he cannot make mistakes. Since the Bible is divinely inspired, it must be without error in everything that its divine and human authors affirm to be true. This means that biblical inerrancy is a mystery even broader in scope than infallibility, which guarantees for us that the Church will always teach the truth concerning faith and morals. Of course the mantle of inerrancy likewise covers faith and morals, but it extends even farther to ensure that all the facts and events of salvation history are accurately presented for us in

---

[1] Hugh of St. Victor, *De arca Noe* 2, 8: PL 176, 642: cf. ibid. 2, 9: PL 176, 642–43.
[2] *DV* 25; cf. Phil 3:8 and St. Jerome, *Commentariorum Isaiam libri xviii*, prol.: PL 24, 17b.

the Scriptures. Inerrancy is our guarantee that the words and deeds of God found in the Bible are unified and true, declaring with one voice the wonders of his saving love.

The guarantee of inerrancy does not mean, however, that the Bible is an all-purpose encyclopedia of information covering every field of study. The Bible is not, for example, a textbook in the empirical sciences, and it should not be treated as one. When biblical authors relate facts of the natural order, we can be sure they are speaking in a purely descriptive and "phenomenological" way, according to the way things appeared to their senses.

Biblical Authority Implicit in these doctrines is God's desire to make himself known to the world and to enter a loving relationship with every man, woman, and child he has created. God gave us the Scriptures not just to inform or motivate us; more than anything he wants to save us. This higher purpose underlies every page of the Bible, indeed every word of it.

In order to reveal himself, God used what theologians call "accommodation". Sometimes the Lord stoops down to communicate by "condescension"—that is, he speaks as humans speak, as if he had the same passions and weakness that we do (for example, God says he was "sorry" that he made man in Genesis 6:6). Other times he communicates by "elevation"—that is, by endowing human words with divine power (for example, through the Prophets). The numerous examples of divine accommodation in the Bible are an expression of God's wise and fatherly ways. For a sensitive father can speak with his children either by condescension, as in baby talk, or by elevation, by bringing a child's understanding up to a more mature level.

God's word is thus saving, fatherly, and personal. Because it speaks directly to us, we must never be indifferent to its content; after all, the word of God is at once the object, cause, and support of our faith. It is, in fact, a test of our faith, since we see in the Scriptures only what faith disposes us to see. If we believe what the Church believes, we will see in Scripture the saving, inerrant, and divinely authored revelation of the Father. If we believe otherwise, we see another book altogether.

This test applies not only to rank-and-file believers but also to the Church's theologians and hierarchy, and even the Magisterium. Vatican II has stressed in recent times that Scripture must be "the very soul of sacred theology" (*Dei Verbum* 24). As Joseph Cardinal Ratzinger, Pope Benedict XVI echoed this powerful teaching with his own, insisting that "the *normative theologians* are the authors of Holy Scripture" (emphasis added). He reminded us that Scripture and the Church's dogmatic teaching are tied tightly together, to the point of being inseparable: "Dogma is by definition nothing other than an interpretation of Scripture." The defined

dogmas of our faith, then, encapsulate the Church's infallible interpretation of Scripture, and theology is a further reflection upon that work.

The Senses of Scripture Because the Bible has both divine and human authors, we are required to master a different sort of reading than we are used to. First, we must read Scripture according to its *literal* sense, as we read any other human literature. At this initial stage, we strive to discover the meaning of the words and expressions used by the biblical writers as they were understood in their original setting and by their original recipients. This means, among other things, that we do not interpret everything we read "literalistically", as though Scripture never speaks in a figurative or symbolic way (it often does!). Rather, we read it according to the rules that govern its different literary forms of writing, depending on whether we are reading a narrative, a poem, a letter, a parable, or an apocalyptic vision. The Church calls us to read the divine books in this way to ensure that we understand what the human authors were laboring to explain to God's people.

The literal sense, however, is not the only sense of Scripture, since we interpret its sacred pages according to the *spiritual* senses as well. In this way, we search out what the Holy Spirit is trying to tell us, beyond even what the human authors have consciously asserted. Whereas the literal sense of Scripture describes a historical reality—a fact, precept, or event—the spiritual senses disclose deeper mysteries revealed through the historical realities. What the soul is to the body, the spiritual senses are to the literal. You can distinguish them; but if you try to separate them, death immediately follows. St. Paul was the first to insist upon this and warn of its consequences: "God ... has qualified us to be ministers of a new covenant, not in a written code but in the Spirit; for the written code kills, but the Spirit gives life" (2 Cor 3:5–6).

Catholic tradition recognizes three spiritual senses that stand upon the foundation of the literal sense of Scripture (see CCC 115). **(1)** The first is the *allegorical* sense, which unveils the spiritual and prophetic meaning of biblical history. Allegorical interpretations thus reveal how persons, events, and institutions of Scripture can point beyond themselves toward greater mysteries yet to come (OT) or display the fruits of mysteries already revealed (NT). Christians have often read the Old Testament in this way to discover how the mystery of Christ in the New Covenant was once hidden in the Old and how the full significance of the Old Covenant was finally made manifest in the New. Allegorical significance is likewise latent in the New Testament, especially in the life and deeds of Jesus recorded in the Gospels. Because Christ is the Head of the Church and the source of her spiritual life, what was accomplished in Christ the Head during his earthly life prefigures what he continually produces in his members through grace. The allegorical sense builds up the virtue of faith. **(2)** The second is the *tropological* or *moral* sense, which reveals how the actions of God's people in the Old Testament and the life of Jesus in the New Testament prompt us to form virtuous habits in our own lives. It therefore draws from Scripture warnings against sin and vice as well as inspirations to pursue holiness and purity. The moral sense is intended to build up the virtue of charity. **(3)** The third is the *anagogical* sense, which points upward to heavenly glory. It shows us how countless events in the Bible prefigure our final union with God in eternity and how things that are "seen" on earth are figures of things "unseen" in heaven. Because the anagogical sense leads us to contemplate our destiny, it is meant to build up the virtue of hope. Together with the literal sense, then, these spiritual senses draw out the fullness of what God wants to give us through his Word and as such comprise what ancient tradition has called the "full sense" of Sacred Scripture.

All of this means that the deeds and events of the Bible are charged with meaning beyond what is immediately apparent to the reader. In essence, that meaning is Jesus Christ and the salvation he died to give us. This is especially true of the books of the New Testament, which proclaim Jesus explicitly; but it is also true of the Old Testament, which speaks of Jesus in more hidden and symbolic ways. The human authors of the Old Testament told us as much as they were able, but they could not clearly discern the shape of all future events standing at such a distance. It is the Bible's divine Author, the Holy Spirit, who could and did foretell the saving work of Christ, from the first page of the Book of Genesis onward.

The New Testament did not, therefore, abolish the Old. Rather, the New fulfilled the Old, and in doing so, it lifted the veil that kept hidden the face of the Lord's bride. Once the veil is removed, we suddenly see the world of the Old Covenant charged with grandeur. Water, fire, clouds, gardens, trees, hills, doves, lambs—all of these things are memorable details in the history and poetry of Israel. But now, seen in the light of Jesus Christ, they are much more. For the Christian with eyes to see, water symbolizes the saving power of Baptism; fire, the Holy Spirit; the spotless lamb, Christ crucified; Jerusalem, the city of heavenly glory.

The spiritual reading of Scripture is nothing new. Indeed, the very first Christians read the Bible this way. St. Paul describes Adam as a "type" that prefigured Jesus Christ (Rom 5:14). A "type" is a real person, place, thing, or event in the Old Testament that foreshadows something greater in the New. From this term we get the word "typology", referring to the study of how the Old Testament prefigures Christ (CCC 128–30). Elsewhere St. Paul draws deeper meanings out of the story of Abraham's sons, declaring, "This is an allegory" (Gal 4:24). He is not suggesting that these events of the distant past never really happened; he is saying that the events both happened *and* signified something more glorious yet to come.

The New Testament later describes the Tabernacle of ancient Israel as "a copy and shadow of the heavenly sanctuary" (Heb 8:5) and the Mosaic Law as a "shadow of the good things to come" (Heb 10:1). St. Peter, in turn, notes that Noah and his family were "saved through water" in a way that "corresponds" to sacramental Baptism, which "now saves you" (1 Pet 3:20–21). It is interesting to note that the expression translated as "corresponds" in this verse is a Greek term that denotes the fulfillment or counterpart of an ancient "type".

We need not look to the apostles, however, to justify a spiritual reading of the Bible. After all, Jesus himself read the Old Testament this way. He referred to Jonah (Mt 12:39), Solomon (Mt 12:42), the Temple (Jn 2:19), and the brazen serpent (Jn 3:14) as "signs" that pointed forward to him. We see in Luke's Gospel, as Christ comforted the disciples on the road to Emmaus, that "beginning with Moses and all the prophets, he interpreted to them in all the Scriptures the things concerning himself" (Lk 24:27). It was precisely this extensive spiritual interpretation of the Old Testament that made such an impact on these once-discouraged travelers, causing their hearts to "burn" within them (Lk 24:32).

Criteria for Biblical Interpretation We, too, must learn to discern the "full sense" of Scripture as it includes both the literal and spiritual senses together. Still, this does not mean we should "read into" the Bible meanings that are not really there. Spiritual exegesis is not an unrestrained flight of the imagination. Rather, it is a sacred science that proceeds according to certain principles and stands accountable to sacred tradition, the Magisterium, and the wider community of biblical interpreters (both living and deceased).

In searching out the full sense of a text, we should always avoid the extreme tendency to "over-spiritualize" in a way that minimizes or denies the Bible's literal truth. St. Thomas Aquinas was well aware of this danger and asserted that "all other senses of Sacred Scripture are based on the literal" (*STh* I, 1, 10, *ad* 1, quoted in CCC 116). On the other hand, we should never confine the meaning of a text to the literal, intended sense of its human author, as if the divine Author did not intend the passage to be read in the light of Christ's coming.

Fortunately the Church has given us guidelines in our study of Scripture. The unique character and divine authorship of the Bible call us to read it "in the Spirit" (*Dei Verbum* 12). Vatican II outlines this teaching in a practical way by directing us to read the Scriptures according to three specific criteria:

9

1. We must "[b]e especially attentive 'to the content and unity of the whole Scripture'" (CCC 112).

2. We must "[r]ead the Scripture within 'the living Tradition of the whole Church'" (CCC 113).

3. We must "[b]e attentive to the analogy of faith" (CCC 114; cf. Rom 12:6).

These criteria protect us from many of the dangers that ensnare readers of the Bible, from the newest inquirer to the most prestigious scholar. Reading Scripture out of context is one such pitfall, and probably the one most difficult to avoid. A memorable cartoon from the 1950s shows a young man poring over the pages of the Bible. He says to his sister: "Don't bother me now; I'm trying to find a Scripture verse to back up one of my preconceived notions." No doubt a biblical text pried from its context can be twisted to say something very different from what its author actually intended.

The Church's criteria guide us here by defining what constitutes the authentic "context" of a given biblical passage. The first criterion directs us to the literary context of every verse, including not only the words and paragraphs that surround it, but also the entire corpus of the biblical author's writings and, indeed, the span of the entire Bible. The *complete* literary context of any Scripture verse includes every text from Genesis to Revelation—because the Bible is a unified book, not just a library of different books. When the Church canonized the Book of Revelation, for example, she recognized it to be incomprehensible apart from the wider context of the entire Bible.

The second criterion places the Bible firmly within the context of a community that treasures a "living tradition". That community is the People of God down through the ages. Christians lived out their faith for well over a millennium before the printing press was invented. For centuries, few believers owned copies of the Gospels, and few people could read anyway. Yet they absorbed the gospel—through the sermons of their bishops and clergy, through prayer and meditation, through Christian art, through liturgical celebrations, and through oral tradition. These were expressions of the one "living tradition", a culture of living faith that stretches from ancient Israel to the contemporary Church. For the early Christians, the gospel could not be understood apart from that tradition. So it is with us. Reverence for the Church's tradition is what protects us from any sort of chronological or cultural provincialism, such as scholarly fads that arise and carry away a generation of interpreters before being dismissed by the next generation.

The third criterion places scriptural texts within the framework of faith. If we believe that the Scriptures are divinely inspired, we must also believe them to be internally coherent and consistent with all the doctrines that Christians believe. Remember, the Church's dogmas (such as the Real Presence, the papacy, the Immaculate Conception)

are not something *added* to Scripture; rather, they are the Church's infallible interpretation *of* Scripture.

Using This Study Guide This volume is designed to lead the reader through Scripture according to the Church's guidelines—faithful to the canon, to the tradition, and to the creeds. The Church's interpretive principles have thus shaped the component parts of this book, and they are designed to make the reader's study as effective and rewarding as possible.

Introductions: We have introduced the biblical book with an essay covering issues such as authorship, date of composition, purpose, and leading themes. This background information will assist readers to approach and understand the text on its own terms.

Annotations: The basic notes at the bottom of every page help the user to read the Scriptures with understanding. They by no means exhaust the meaning of the sacred text but provide background material to help the reader make sense of what he reads. Often these notes make explicit what the sacred writers assumed or held to be implicit. They also provide a great deal of historical, cultural, geographical, and theological information pertinent to the inspired narratives—information that can help the reader bridge the distance between the biblical world and his own.

Cross-References: Between the biblical text at the top of each page and the annotations at the bottom, numerous references are listed to point readers to other scriptural passages related to the one being studied. This follow-up is an essential part of any serious study. It is also an excellent way to discover how the content of Scripture "hangs together" in a providential unity. Along with biblical cross-references, the annotations refer to select paragraphs from the *Catechism of the Catholic Church*. These are not doctrinal "proof texts" but are designed to help the reader interpret the Bible in accordance with the mind of the Church. The *Catechism* references listed either handle the biblical text directly or treat a broader doctrinal theme that sheds significant light on that text.

Topical Essays, Word Studies, Charts: These features bring readers to a deeper understanding of select details. The *topical essays* take up major themes and explain them more thoroughly and theologically than the annotations, often relating them to the doctrines of the Church. Occasionally the annotations are supplemented by *word studies* that put readers in touch with the ancient languages of Scripture. These should help readers to understand better and appreciate the inspired terminology that runs throughout the sacred books. Also included are various *charts* that summarize biblical information "at a glance".

Icon Annotations: Three distinctive icons are interspersed throughout the annotations, each one corresponding to one of the Church's three criteria for biblical interpretation. Bullets indicate the passage or passages to which these icons apply.

Notes marked by the book icon relate to the "content and unity" of Scripture, showing how particular passages of the Old Testament illuminate the mysteries of the New. Much of the information in these notes explains the original context of the citations and indicates how and why this has a direct bearing on Christ or the Church. Through these notes, the reader can develop a sensitivity to the beauty and unity of God's saving plan as it stretches across both Testaments.

Notes marked by the dove icon examine particular passages in light of the Church's "living tradition". Because the Holy Spirit both guides the Magisterium and inspires the spiritual senses of Scripture, these annotations supply information along both of these lines. On the one hand, they refer to the Church's doctrinal teaching as presented by various popes, creeds, and ecumenical councils; on the other, they draw from (and paraphrase) the spiritual interpretations of various Fathers, Doctors, and saints.

Notes marked by the keys icon pertain to the "analogy of faith". Here we spell out how the mysteries of our faith "unlock" and explain one another. This type of comparison between Christian beliefs displays the coherence and unity of defined dogmas, which are the Church's infallible interpretations of Scripture.

Putting It All in Perspective Perhaps the most important context of all we have saved for last: the interior life of the individual reader. What we get out of the Bible will largely depend on how we approach the Bible. Unless we are living a sustained and disciplined life of prayer, we will never have the reverence, the profound humility, or the grace we need to see the Scriptures for what they really are.

You are approaching the "word of God". But for thousands of years, since before he knit you in your mother's womb, the Word of God has been approaching you.

One Final Note. The volume you hold in your hands is only a small part of a much larger work still in production. Study helps similar to those printed in this booklet are being prepared for *all* the books of the Bible and will appear gradually as they are finished. Our ultimate goal is to publish a single, one-volume Study Bible that will include the entire text of Scripture, along with all the annotations, charts, cross-references, maps, and other features found in the following pages. Individual booklets will be published in the meantime, with the hope that God's people can begin to benefit from this labor before its full completion.

We have included a long list of Study Questions in the back to make this format as useful as possible, not only for individual study, but for group settings and discussions as well. The questions are designed to help readers both "understand" the Bible and "apply" it to their lives. We pray that God will make use of our efforts and yours to help renew the face of the earth! «

INTRODUCTION TO JOSHUA

Author and Date Little is known for certain about the origin of the Book of Joshua. Jewish tradition credits the work to Joshua himself, with the notice of his death in 24:29–31 being ascribed to his contemporary, Eleazar the priest (Babylonian Talmud, *Baba Bathra* 15a). It is true that Joshua stands out as the main character in the story and that Joshua appears therein as someone who could read and write (8:32; 24:26). Nevertheless, the book makes no explicit claim to be written by him. The Book of Joshua is both formally anonymous and somewhat ambiguous about the time of its composition.

Limited information about the authorship and age of the book may be gleaned from its contents. On the one hand, parts of the book clearly *postdate* the lifetime of Joshua, such as the reference to the Danite migration (19:47), an event that took place in the days of the Judges (Judg 18:27–29), along with a reference to "the elders who outlived Joshua" (24:31). One can also point to several passages where circumstances described in the story are said to have remained unchanged at the time the author was writing (see the recurring phrase "to this day" in 4:9; 5:9; 6:25; 7:26; 8:28–29; 9:27; 10:27; 13:13; 14:14; 15:63; 16:10). It is impossible to say from this expression how much time elapsed between the circumstances in the story and the author's comments in hindsight, but many think that an appreciable historical distance is implied.

On the other hand, further parts of the book appear to *predate* the rise of the Davidic monarchy at the turn of the first millennium B.C. Most of these appear in the topographical lists of chapters 13–21. For instance, the author is writing at a time when the Jebusites held power in Jerusalem (15:63), and yet David conquered the Jebusites and claimed the city for Israel around 1004 B.C. (2 Sam 5:6–10). Similarly, the author remarks that Canaanites were dwelling in Gezer at the time of composition (16:10), and yet the Canaanite population of Gezer was annihilated by Egyptian forces during the reign of Solomon in the tenth century B.C. (1 Kings 9:16). Furthermore, the author refers to certain Canaanite towns using ancient names that were no longer in use during most of Israel's history (e.g., "Kiriath-arba" for Hebron, 14:15; "Baalah" for Kiriath-jearim, 15:9; "Jebus" for Jerusalem, 18:28). Information of this sort has led a few scholars to suppose that the author had access to the roster of towns and territories drawn up by Israelite surveyors in the time of Joshua himself (see 18:2–9).

Modern critical scholarship, while recognizing some archaic features and traditions in Joshua, maintains that the current form of the book dates to the Babylonian Exile in the sixth century B.C. The argument is that Joshua has conspicuously close ties with the biblical books that follow, namely, Judges, 1–2 Samuel, and 1–2 Kings. These writings not only form a continuous plotline of Israel's life in the Promised Land, they also employ characteristic idioms and share a common theological outlook to such an extent that many believe they were edited together as a group after Judah's deportation to Babylon in 586 (narrated in 2 Kings 25). Scholars have come to designate this collection of books from Joshua to 2 Kings (minus Ruth) as "the Deuteronomistic History" because together they view Israel's national story through the prism of Deuteronomy.

Giving all these considerations due weight, it is probable that the Book of Joshua appeared in more than one edition before reaching its final, canonical form. The first efforts at gathering traditions about Joshua and the Conquest into a connected narrative seem to have taken place during the *settlement period* between Joshua and David (before 1000 B.C.). Some or even most of this material could be based on recollections going back to Joshua and his contemporaries. Nevertheless, the final form of the book may well have crystallized during the *exilic period* between the collapse of the kingdom of Judah and the rebuilding of a Jewish commonwealth in Israel (during the 500s B.C.). This would account for the internal data of the book reasonably well, given the limitations of our knowledge. Still, there are numerous modern scholars who date the first edition (or redaction) of the Book of Joshua, not to the pre-monarchical period, but to the reign of King Josiah (640 to 609 B.C.), mainly because of a critical preference to trace the origin of the Book of Deuteronomy to this time. Since all agree that Joshua appears to be indebted to Deuteronomy, the date one assigns to the latter has a direct bearing on how one dates the compositional stages of the former.

Title The book is named after its leading character, Joshua the son of Nun. Everywhere he stands at the center of the action as the successor to Moses, the shepherd of Israel, and the anointed warrior of Yahweh. His birth name was Hoshea, meaning "salvation", but later Moses expanded it to *Yehoshua*, or Joshua, meaning "Yahweh is salvation" (Num 13:16). The Greek Septuagint (LXX) renders this name *Iēsous*, which is translatable either as "Joshua" or "Jesus". The Latin Vulgate supplies the heading *Liber Iosue*, "Book of Joshua".

Place in the Canon The Book of Joshua follows immediately after the Pentateuch because it picks up the thread of the story going forward from the death of Moses (Deut 34:5–8). In the Hebrew Bible, it is the first of the "Former Prophets", the name given to Joshua, Judges, Samuel, and Kings. The idea is not that these books are concerned with predicting future events; rather, they look at history from a prophetic perspective, that is, with attention given to God's interventions in history as well as the meaning he invests in those events. Likewise, a few of the outstanding figures in these stories are viewed in the Bible as prophetic figures (for example, Joshua, Samuel, David, Elijah). Christian tradition considers Joshua to be one of the "Historical Books" of the Old Testament, without denying its prophetic character.

Structure The Book of Joshua follows a simple, fourfold outline. **(1)** Chapters 1–5 relate the circumstances of Israel's crossing into Canaan from east of the Jordan. **(2)** Chapters 6–12 describe the subjugation of Canaan by the united armies of Israel under the command of Joshua. **(3)** Chapters 13–21 delineate how the land and cities of Canaan are parceled out to the incoming tribes. **(4)** Chapters 22–24 give a report of Joshua's farewell address to the people, ending with a series of short notices about the burial of Joshua, Joseph, and Eleazar. See also *Outline*.

Themes The Book of Joshua narrates Israel's dramatic entrance into the Promised Land. From beginning to end, from the preparations for invasion until the assignment of tribal territories after the dust of war settles, the attention of the reader is fixed on the land as it passes into the hands of the People of God. This epic account of the Conquest of Canaan can be analyzed on multiple levels.

(1) *Theologically*, Israel's capture of Canaan is the fulfillment of a divine oath sworn to Abraham centuries earlier. Yahweh had pledged, by a covenant of grant, that Abraham's descendants would someday possess the land of Canaan and dispossess the nations that lived there (Gen 15:18–21; 17:8). Hope in this divine promise dominated much of the patriarchal (Gen 26:3; 28:4, 13; 35:12) and Exodus narratives (Ex 3:8; 6:8; 13:5; 23:23–33, etc.) of the Pentateuch. In Joshua, the land of promise finally becomes Israel's possession (21:43). Yahweh honors his covenant by leading the attack on Canaan as a divine Warrior, who fights for his people and ensures their success (10:14; 23:10; 24:11–12). He opens the way into Canaan by holding back the waters of the Jordan (3:11–13); he sends an angelic army to fight alongside Israel (5:13–15); he pounds enemy forces with hailstones from the sky (10:11); and he holds the sun still at Gibeon so that Israel can accomplish its mission (10:12–14). In these and other ways, the God of Israel features as one of the main actors in the Book of Joshua.

(2) *Militarily*, Israel launches its effort to subdue the land of Canaan in three phases. The first is the *central* campaign (chaps. 6–8), which sees the walled fortress of Jericho fall to Israelite conquerors, followed by Ai, and then the central highlands. The second phase is the *southern* campaign (chap. 10), where Joshua and his men rout an alliance of Amorite kings and claim lordship over cities and lands in the south. The third phase is the *northern* campaign (chap. 11), where the armies of Israel vanquish a coalition of Galilean cities that have joined forces to halt the Israelite advance. Brief mention is also made of victories in other localities (12:13–18, 21–24). Together these inaugural triumphs combine to give Israel a decisive claim to a new homeland. For questions about the moral and theological validity of Israel's warfare, see essay: *The Conquest of Canaan* at Josh 6.

(3) *Canonically*, the Book of Joshua presents a picture of Canaan's occupation quite distinct from what appears in the Book of Judges. Critical scholarship has often set the two accounts in opposition, declaring Joshua to be an idealized report of events and Judges to be the more accurate and realistic version. It is said that Joshua presents the tribes of Israel acting in unison and marching invincibly through the land, with the seizure and settlement of Canaan all but complete by the end of the book, whereas Judges presents Israel divided in its efforts to claim the land, causing a drawn-out struggle that witnesses many setbacks stretching over numerous generations. There is a degree of truth in these observations, but the alleged conflict is more apparent than real. In point of fact, there is little historical overlap between the narratives of Joshua and Judges. They present, not two versions of the same story, but two distinct phases of a much longer story. Joshua tells only of the initial raids that gave Israel a foothold in the land, establishing a base from which to extend its control by future campaigns (23:4–5). The book makes no actual claim that the totality of Canaan was captured by Israel soon after its arrival. A few comments can be singled out that use stereotypical and triumphalist rhetoric (10:40–42; 11:23), such as one finds in other military chronicles of the ancient Near East, but the book openly acknowledges that much of the land and many of its cities remain unconquered in the days of Joshua (see 13:1–7; 15:63; 16:10; 17:11–13, 16–18). This does not contradict the report given in Judges; rather, it sets the stage for the many challenges that an incomplete Conquest would pose to Israel in the next phase of the story, which is the main focus of Judges.

(4) *Chronologically*, Israel crossed into Canaan forty years after its Exodus out of Egypt. Since scholarship disagrees about the date of the Exodus, there is a corresponding disagreement over the date of the Conquest, which some put about 1406 B.C. and others about 1220 B.C. (see essay: *The Date of the*

Exodus at Ex 11). Unfortunately, on this question, archaeology can sometimes be more of a complicating factor than a clarifying one. Evidence from excavations in Israel is often said to favor a conquest in the late thirteenth century, at which time sites such as Bethel, Lachish, Debir, and Hazor were violently destroyed. But these findings fall short of confirming the later date, not least because the biblical account of the Conquest indicates that Israel engaged in very limited destruction of property. Only three cities—Jericho, Ai, and Hazor—were put to the torch, according to 6:24; 8:19; 11:11–13. Indeed, the supposition that archaeology should expect to find signs of mass devastation throughout Palestine overlooks the fact that Israel had every reason to keep the physical infrastructure of the country more or less intact. This is because God had promised to give his people the dwellings and farmsteads of the Canaanites to be their own (24:13; Deut 6:10–11; 19:1–2). Other challenges to fixing the date of the Conquest by archaeology include disputes about the proper identification of excavated settlements (especially Ai), significant erosion at critical sites (especially Jericho), and multiple layers of destruction at sites that align with more than one proposed date (especially Hazor). Consequently, the evidence of archaeology remains ambiguous enough to support more than one position on the date of the Conquest.

(5) *Historically*, Israel's emergence in Canaan has been explained in different ways by different scholars. Serious doubts concerning the historical trustworthiness of the Bible, along with disagreements over the interpretation of archaeological findings, has given birth to contemporary "models" that offer alternative explanations for the origins of Israel in the land. Some envision a *peaceful infiltration* of Canaan that involved a gradual and nonviolent influx of nomadic peoples into Canaan who professed allegiance to a common deity known as Yahweh. Others theorize that a *peasant revolt* was instigated by the rural population of Canaan, who overthrew their oppressive urban monarchs, in part through an alliance with liberated slaves coming from Egypt. Still others advocate a model of *Palestinian unification* in which the indigenous population of Canaan coalesced into an agricultural society that, over time, developed into a nation bonded together by religious ideals. Unfortunately, these models are highly speculative constructs. Beyond that, they stand in fairly serious conflict with the Bible's version of Israel's ethnic origin and military takeover of Canaan. Whatever added light these models may be said to throw on the circumstances surrounding Israel's settlement in Canaan, most still agree that a complete repudiation of the biblical account is not warranted on either literary, historical, or archaeological grounds.

Christian Perspective Tradition reads the story of Joshua with reference to Christ and the Church. Joshua typifies Jesus as the captain of the covenant people. Not only does he bear the name of the Savior in advance (in the Greek Scriptures, both names are spelled *Iēsous*), but he triumphs over the enemies of God's people and leads them safely into their blessed inheritance. The Promised Land of Canaan has layers of spiritual significance. *Allegorically*, Canaan is the world that is conquered by Christ leading and directing the missionary efforts of the Church. Battles for conversion are fought and won, not with the physical implements of war, but with the sword of the Spirit, which is the word of God. *Morally*, Canaan is the soul of the believer that is captured and claimed by Jesus. As the new Joshua, he drives from it, not a host of wicked nations, but a host of sins and vices that drag us away from the Lord. *Anagogically*, Canaan is our heavenly homeland. There the saints find rest from the grueling wilderness of this world and enjoy forever the milk and honey of eternal happiness (CCC 117).

OUTLINE OF JOSHUA

1. **The Entrance into Canaan (chaps. 1–5)**
    A. Preparations for Invasion (chaps. 1–2)
    B. The Crossing of the Jordan (chaps. 3–5)

2. **The Conquest of Canaan (chaps. 6–12)**
    A. The Fall of Jericho and Ai (chaps. 6–8)
    B. Covenant with the Gibeonites (chap. 9)
    C. The Southern Campaign (chap. 10)
    D. The Northern Campaign (chap. 11)
    E. Kings Conquered by Moses and Joshua (chap. 12)

3. **The Division of Canaan (chaps. 13–21)**
    A. Unconquered Territory (13:1–7)
    B. Eastern Lands of Reuben, Gad, and Half-Manasseh (13:8–33)
    C. Western Lands Given to Judah, Ephraim, and Half-Manasseh (chaps. 14–17)
    D. Western Lands Given to the Remaining Seven Tribes (chaps. 18–19)
    E. The Six Cities of Refuge (chap. 20)
    F. The 48 Levitical Cities (chap. 21)

4. **The Farewell Speeches of Joshua (chaps. 22–24)**
    A. The Altar of Witness (chap. 22)
    B. Joshua's Farewell Address (chap. 23)
    C. Covenant Renewal at Shechem (chap. 24)

THE BOOK OF

JOSHUA

God Commissions Joshua

1 After the death of Moses the servant of the Lord, the Lord said to Joshua the son of Nun, Moses' minister, [2] "Moses my servant is dead; now therefore arise, go over this Jordan, you and all this people, into the land which I am giving to them, to the sons of Israel. [3] Every place that the sole of your foot will tread upon I have given to you, as I promised to Moses. [4] From the wilderness and this Lebanon as far as the great river, the river Euphrates, all the land of the Hittites to the Great Sea toward the going down of the sun shall be your territory. [5] No man shall be able to stand before you all the days of your life; as I was with Moses, so I will be with you; I will not fail you or forsake you. [6] Be strong and of good courage; for you shall cause this people to inherit the land which I swore to their fathers to give them. [7] Only be strong and very courageous, being careful to do according to all the law which Moses my servant commanded you; turn not from it to the right hand or to the left, that you may have good success wherever you go. [8] This book of the law shall not depart out of your mouth, but you shall meditate on it day and night, that you may be careful to do according to all that is written in it; for then you shall make your way prosperous, and then you shall have good success. [9] Have I not commanded you? Be strong and of good courage; be not frightened, neither be dismayed; for the Lord your God is with you wherever you go."

Preparations for Taking Over the Land

10 Then Joshua commanded the officers of the people, [11] "Pass through the camp, and command the people, 'Prepare your provisions; for within

---

1:5: Heb 13:5.

1:1 death of Moses: Narrated in Deut 34:1–8. The Book of Joshua begins soon after his passing in the 40th year of the Exodus. **servant of the Lord:** An honorary title later given to Joshua (24:29). **Joshua:** Given the reins of spiritual leadership as the successor of Moses. Together with Caleb, he is the only survivor of the Exodus generation that left Egypt who will enter Canaan (Num 14:29–30). Passage into the land is the reward for his heroic faith (Num 14:6–9; 32:11–12). See note on Num 27:18. • *Allegorically*, Joshua is a type of the Lord Jesus, not only because of his name, but also because of his work. In crossing the Jordan, subduing enemy kingdoms, and dividing the land among his people, we see in symbol how Jesus marked out the spiritual realm of the Church, which is the heavenly Jerusalem (St. Jerome, *Letters* 53, 8). Joshua succeeded Moses to show in advance that the New Law of Christ would succeed the Old Law given through Moses (Lactantius, *Divine Institutes* 4, 17).

1:2 over this Jordan: Israel is encamped on the plains of Moab, east of the Jordan. The land of Canaan lies west of the river. According to the biblical narrative, the people have been stationed on the plains of Moab since Num 22:1. **I am giving:** The land is primarily a "gift" that God is giving to Israel; only secondarily is it something to be taken by conquest. This point is emphasized in the opening chapter (1:3, 6, 11, 13, 15).

1:3 your foot: The Hebrew for "your" is plural and thus refers to the Israelites.

1:4 your territory: The land promised to Israel is much larger than the land conquered under Joshua. The scope of this wider territory, stretching from the Mediterranean coast (the Great Sea) to the border of Mesopotamia (the river Euphra-tes), was not under Israelite control until the reign of King Solomon (1 Kings 4:21). For similar passages that delineate the full dimensions of the Promised Land, see Gen 15:18–21, Ex 23:31, and Deut 1:6–8.

1:5 with Moses ... with you: Joshua is graced with the same divine presence that enabled Moses to fulfill his mission. • Joshua plays the part of a new Moses throughout the book. Mosaic typology is grounded on explicit statements as well as implicit suggestions that highlight the similarities between Joshua and his forebear. **(1)** Joshua receives the same allegiance that Israel once gave to Moses (1:17; 4:14). **(2)** Joshua urges the people to sanctify themselves in preparation for divine miracles (3:5) just as Moses once urged Israel to prepare itself for divine instruction (Ex 19:10–11, 14–15). **(3)** Joshua sends spies into Canaan (2:1; 7:2) just as Moses did years earlier (Num 13:2, 17). **(4)** Joshua leads Israel across the dry riverbed of the Jordan (3:14–17; 4:23), recalling how Moses led the people over a dry path through the sea (Ex 14:16, 21–22). **(5)** Joshua removes his sandals on holy ground (5:16) just as Moses did at the burning bush (Ex 3:5). **(6)** The battlefield victories of Joshua west of the Jordan (12:7–24) parallel the triumphs of Moses east of the Jordan (12:1–6). **(7)** Joshua speaks the words of Yahweh to the people (4:1–7, 15–17, etc.) just as Moses spoke divine instructions to Israel (Ex 19:3–7; 24:3; 33:1–4, etc.). **(8)** Joshua stretches forth his hand to give Israel victory in battle (8:26) just as Moses extended his arms in prayer for the same purpose (Ex 17:11–13). **(9)** Joshua is honored at the end of his life with the title "servant of the Lord" (24:29), the same title given to Moses throughout the book (1:1, 13; 8:31, 33; 11:12, etc.).

1:8 book of the law: The Book of Deuteronomy, which Moses wrote on a scroll and placed "by the side of" the Ark of the Covenant, according to Deut 31:26. **meditate on it:** Reflection on the Torah and taking its lessons to heart are a means of spiritual formation (Ps 1:1–3).

1:9 be not frightened: Recalls how fear blocked Israel's entrance into Canaan almost 40 years earlier, although Joshua himself showed exceptional courage on the occasion (Num 14:8–9).

This book continues the narrative from the death of Moses (Deut 34), through the conquest of Canaan, down to the great covenant-renewal at Shechem. The account of the conquest is stylized and summarized: thus, not all the tribes entered the land together as here described, the operation was not so free of difficulties and even failures as we might assume after a reading of this book, and the occupation of the whole country could not have been carried out by Joshua in person. Judges 1 gives a somewhat different and complementary version.

three days you are to pass over this Jordan, to go in to take possession of the land which the LORD your God gives you to possess.'"

12 And to the Reubenites, the Gadites, and the half-tribe of Manas′seh Joshua said, 13"Remember the word which Moses the servant of the LORD commanded you, saying, 'The LORD your God is providing you a place of rest, and will give you this land.' 14Your wives, your little ones, and your cattle shall remain in the land which Moses gave you beyond the Jordan; but all the men of valor among you shall pass over armed before your brethren and shall help them, 15until the LORD gives rest to your brethren as well as to you, and they also take possession of the land which the LORD your God is giving them; then you shall return to the land of your possession, and shall possess it, the land which Moses the servant of the LORD gave you beyond the Jordan toward the sunrise." 16And they answered Joshua, "All that you have commanded us we will do, and wherever you send us we will go. 17Just as we obeyed Moses in all things, so we will obey you; only may the LORD your God be with you, as he was with Moses! 18Whoever rebels against your

commandment and disobeys your words, whatever you command him, shall be put to death. Only be strong and of good courage."

Spies Sent to Jericho

2 And Joshua the son of Nun sent two men secretly from Shittim as spies, saying, "Go, view the land, especially Jericho." And they went, and came into the house of a harlot whose name was Ra′hab, and lodged there. 2And it was told the king of Jericho, "Behold, certain men of Israel have come here tonight to search out the land." 3Then the king of Jericho sent to Ra′hab, saying, "Bring forth the men that have come to you, who entered your house; for they have come to search out all the land." 4But the woman had taken the two men and hidden them; and she said, "True, men came to me, but I did not know where they came from; 5and when the gate was to be closed, at dark, the men went out; where the men went I do not know; pursue them quickly, for you will overtake them." 6But she had brought them up to the roof, and hid them with the stalks of flax which she had laid in order on the roof. 7So the men pursued after them on the way to the Jordan as far as the fords;

1:12–18: Josh 22:1–34; Num 32:20–22.

1:12–18 Joshua confirms the pledge of Reuben, Gad, and Manasseh to join the war effort in Canaan before settling down with their families east of the Jordan (Num 32:1–42). **1:13 place of rest:** Israel will enjoy the Lord's peace and protection in Canaan once the land is secured. This new era will follow on the heels of forty years of wandering in the desert (Num 14:34) in addition to prolonged oppression in Egypt before that (Gen 15:13; Ex 1:8–14). Mention is made of this "rest" several times in Joshua (1:15; 11:23; 21:44; 22:4; 23:1). • In the Book of Hebrews, the rest that Joshua gives the people in Canaan is a sign of the eternal rest that Jesus, a new Joshua, promises the faithful (Heb 4:1–10; 11:13–16). See introduction: *Christian Perspective.*

2:1–24 The inspection of Jericho. Located at modern Tell es-Sultan, the city stood six miles north of the Dead Sea overlooking a fertile oasis in the western Jordan valley. It was built on a protective mound, encircled by a fortified wall, and stood as the first major obstacle to Israel's possession of Canaan. Jericho is one of the oldest settlements known to history, with traces of human occupation stretching back into the Mesolithic period (between ca. 9000 and 8700 B.C.). Archaeological excavations at Jericho have unearthed signs of mass devastation and burning, along with an outward collapse of the city's main defensive wall, that are dated to the middle of the second millennium B.C. However, experts disagree over whether Jericho's demise took place at the end of the Middle Bronze Age (ca. 1550) or the Late Bronze Age (ca. 1400). Interpretation of the evidence is complicated by severe erosion at the site as well as the fact that only small segments of the mound have been examined.

2:1 Shittim: The final wilderness encampment of the Israelites. It was located on the plains of Moab, northeast of the Dead Sea (Num 33:49). **spies:** Sent to gather military intelligence before the battle of Jericho. **harlot:** The Hebrew refers to a "prostitute". Jewish tradition stretching back to NT times considered Rahab an innkeeper or perhaps a barmaid (Josephus, *Antiquities* 5, 8). **Rahab:** A Canaanite convert to the faith of Israel, as seen in her acceptance of Yahweh in 2:11 (echoing Deut 4:39). By helping the

spies and negotiating a covenant of peace and protection for her family (2:12–21), she escapes the devastation of Jericho and finds a place among the people of God (6:22–25). • The NT designates Rahab an ancestress of Jesus (Mt 1:5) and a heroine who exemplifies Christian teaching on faith made active in good works (Heb 11:31; Jas 2:25–26). • *Allegorically*, Rahab is a type of the Church, which takes in souls endangered by pride and lets them out by another route, the way of humility and patience (Cassiodorus, *Exposition on the Psalms* 86, 4).

2:2 king of Jericho: Canaan was made up of multiple city-states ruled by local monarchs. This is reflected in the list of conquered kings in 12:7–24 as well as in the *Amarna Letters* discovered in Egypt in the late 19th century. These letters were part of a royal archive of texts that included correspondence between Egypt and the kings of Syria and Palestine from the 14th century B.C. In several letters, Canaanite rulers appeal to the Pharaoh for help in dealing with landless mercenaries and marauders called *habiru* or *'apiru*. It is possible, according to some scholars, that the incoming Israelites were viewed as part of this disruptive horde, although the *habiru* of the letters and the biblical "Hebrews" cannot simply be equated.

2:5 the men went out: False information is fed to the king to provide for the escape of the spies. Scripture praises Rahab for her faith and hospitality, but not for her deceptive ploy. Her resort to this measure is narrated but is not thereby condoned. • Catholic moral theology, in agreement with Paul (Rom 3:8), insists that evil may never be done that good may result from it (CCC 1789). • Nothing contrary to the truth can be just. Therefore no lie can be just. When examples of lying are put forward in Scripture, either they are misunderstood to be lies or, if genuine, they are not to be imitated. In the case of the Hebrew midwives and Rahab of Jericho, God deals well with them, not because they lie, but because they are merciful to his people (St. Augustine, *Against Lying* 15, 31–32).

2:6 flax: Harvested in spring and used to make linen. Its stalks were soaked and spread out on rooftops to dry in the hot sun.

and as soon as the pursuers had gone out, the gate was shut.

8 Before they lay down, she came up to them on the roof, ⁹and said to the men, "I know that the Lᴏʀᴅ has given you the land, and that the fear of you has fallen upon us, and that all the inhabitants of the land melt away before you. ¹⁰For we have heard how the Lᴏʀᴅ dried up the water of the Red Sea before you when you came out of Egypt, and what you did to the two kings of the Am′orites that were beyond the Jordan, to Si′hon and Og, whom you utterly destroyed. ¹¹And as soon as we heard it, our hearts melted, and there was no courage left in any man, because of you; for the Lᴏʀᴅ your God is he who is God in heaven above and on earth beneath. ¹²Now then, swear to me by the Lᴏʀᴅ that as I have dealt kindly with you, you also will deal kindly with my father's house, and give me a sure sign, ¹³and save alive my father and mother, my brothers and sisters, and all who belong to them, and deliver our lives from death." ¹⁴And the men said to her, "Our life for yours! If you do not tell this business of ours, then we will deal kindly and faithfully with you when the Lᴏʀᴅ gives us the land."

15 Then she let them down by a rope through the window, for her house was built into the city wall, so that she dwelt in the wall. ¹⁶And she said to them, "Go into the hills, lest the pursuers meet you; and hide yourselves there three days, until the pursuers have returned; then afterward you may go your way." ¹⁷The men said to her, "We will be guiltless with respect to this oath of yours which you have made us swear. ¹⁸Behold, when we come into the land, you shall bind this scarlet cord in the window through which you let us down; and you shall gather into your house your father and mother, your brothers, and all your father's household. ¹⁹If any one goes out of the doors of your house into the street, his blood shall be upon his head, and we shall be guiltless; but if a hand is laid upon any one who is with you in the house, his blood shall be on our head. ²⁰But if you tell this business of ours, then we shall be guiltless with respect to your oath which you have made us swear." ²¹And she said, "According to your words, so be it." Then she sent them away, and they departed; and she bound the scarlet cord in the window.

22 They departed, and went into the hills, and remained there three days, until the pursuers returned; for the pursuers had made search all along the way and found nothing. ²³Then the two men came down again from the hills, and passed over and came to Joshua the son of Nun; and they told him all that had befallen them. ²⁴And they said to Joshua, "Truly the Lᴏʀᴅ has given all the land into our hands; and moreover all the inhabitants of the land are fainthearted because of us."

Israel Passes over the Jordan

3 Early in the morning Joshua rose and set out from Shittim, with all the sons of Israel; and they came to the Jordan, and lodged there before they passed over. ²At the end of three days the officers went through the camp ³and commanded the people, "When you see the ark of the covenant

---

2:10 Sihon and Og: Former kings from east of the Jordan who were vanquished by the Israelites under the command of Moses (Num 21:21–35).

2:14 Our life for yours!: An ancient oath formula (2:17). The spies put themselves under a conditional curse of death should anyone from Rahab's family die in the violent overthrow of the city (2:19).

2:15 dwelt in the wall: Above the lower revetment wall around Jericho, which supported a paved rampart, archaeologists discovered simple dwellings adjacent to the defensive wall. Escaping through windows in the outer wall was necessary once the gates of the city had been closed for the night (2:5). The apostle Paul once evaded pursuers by making a similar nighttime escape from the walled city of Damascus (Acts 9:25; 2 Cor 11:32–33).

2:16 Go into the hills: Rahab sends the spies westward into the hill country, knowing that the search party has gone eastward toward the Jordan (2:7).

2:18 scarlet cord: A sign of protection, much like the blood streaked on the doorways of Israelite homes at Passover (see Ex 12:22–23). • *Allegorically,* the mystery of the Lord's blood is signified by the color of the cord, and Rahab herself is a type of the Church saved from destruction (St. Jerome, *Letters* 52, 3). The red cord, tied in the window of the harlot, is a symbol of the blood of Christ, by which sinners and fornicators from every nation are redeemed (St. Justin Martyr, *Dialogue with Trypho* 111).

3:1—5:1 Israel crosses the Jordan into Canaan. • The narrative is worded to evoke memories of the Exodus. **(1)** The Lord leads "the way" into Canaan, enthroned on the Ark of the Covenant (3:3–4), just as he led "the way" out of Egypt, appearing in a pillar of cloud and fire (Ex 13:21). **(2)** Israel passes over the Jordan on "dry ground" (3:17), calling to mind how the people passed through the sea on "dry land" (Ex 14:21). **(3)** Yahweh piles up the waters of the Jordan in a "heap" (3:16), just as the waters rose in a "heap" along the path through the sea (Ex 15:8). **(4)** Israel marches into Canaan "in haste" (4:10) much as Israel streamed out of Egypt "in haste" on the night of deliverance (Ex 12:33). **(5)** News of the Jordan crossing causes the Canaanites to melt with fear (5:1), mirroring how news of the sea crossing caused the Canaanites and their neighbors to do the same (Ex 15:14–16). For parallels between Joshua and Moses, see note on 1:5. • *Morally,* the crossing of the Jordan teaches us to leave behind the desert of sin, to hasten through the waters to the land fruitful with joy, and to destroy the Jericho of our former way of life that it might never be rebuilt (St. Gregory of Nyssa, *On the Baptism of Jesus*).

3:1 Shittim: On the plains of Moab. See note on 2:1. **the Jordan:** Originates in the foothills of Mount Hermon, flows south through the Sea of Galilee, and empties into the Dead Sea. Its winding course formed the eastern border of Canaan (Num 33:51).

3:3 ark of the covenant: Represents the throne of Yahweh (Is 37:16) as well as his battle chariot (1 Chron 28:18). It was the focal point of Israelite worship as well as an instrument of Israelite warfare (Num 10:33–36; 1 Sam 4:3–4). The prominent role of the Ark in Joshua shows that the Conquest was as much a liturgical event as a military operation (6:8–11). For the shape and dimensions of the Ark, see notes on Ex 25:10 and 25:18.

of the LORD your God being carried by the Levitical priests, then you shall set out from your place and follow it, [4]that you may know the way you shall go, for you have not passed this way before. Yet there shall be a space between you and it, a distance of about two thousand cubits; do not come near it." [5]And Joshua said to the people, "Sanctify yourselves; for tomorrow the LORD will do wonders among you." [6]And Joshua said to the priests, "Take up the ark of the covenant, and pass on before the people." And they took up the ark of the covenant, and went before the people.

[7] And the LORD said to Joshua, "This day I will begin to exalt you in the sight of all Israel, that they may know that, as I was with Moses, so I will be with you. [8]And you shall command the priests who bear the ark of the covenant, 'When you come to the brink of the waters of the Jordan, you shall stand still in the Jordan.'" [9]And Joshua said to the sons of Israel, "Come here, and hear the words of the LORD your God." [10]And Joshua said, "Hereby you shall know that the living God is among you, and that he will without fail drive out from before you the Canaanites, the Hittites, the Hi'vites, the Per'izzites, the Gir'gashites, the Am'orites, and the Jeb'usites. [11]Behold, the ark of the covenant of the Lord of all the earth is to pass over before you into the Jordan. [12]Now therefore take twelve men from the tribes of Israel, from each tribe a man. [13]And when the soles of the feet of the priests who bear the ark of the LORD, the Lord of all the earth, shall rest in the waters of the Jordan, the waters of the Jordan shall be stopped from flowing, and the waters coming down from above shall stand in one heap."

[14] So, when the people set out from their tents, to pass over the Jordan with the priests bearing the ark of the covenant before the people, [15]and when those who bore the ark had come to the Jordan, and the feet of the priests bearing the ark were dipped in the brink of the water (the Jordan overflows all its banks throughout the time of harvest), [16]the waters coming down from above stood and rose up in a heap far off, at Adam, the city that is beside Zar'ethan, and those flowing down toward the sea of the Ar'abah, the Salt Sea, were wholly cut off; and the people passed over opposite Jericho. [17]And while all Israel were passing over on dry ground, the priests who bore the ark of the covenant of the LORD stood on dry ground in the midst of the Jordan, until all the nation finished passing over the Jordan.*

Twelve Stones Set Up at Gilgal

4 When all the nation had finished passing over the Jordan, the LORD said to Joshua, [2]"Take twelve men from the people, from each tribe a man, [3]and command them, 'Take twelve stones from here out of the midst of the Jordan, from the very place where the priests' feet stood, and carry them over with you, and lay them down in the place where you lodge tonight.'" [4]Then Joshua called the twelve men from the sons of Israel, whom he had appointed, a man from each tribe; [5]and Joshua said to them, "Pass on before the ark of the LORD your God into the midst of the Jordan, and take up each of you a stone upon his shoulder, according to the number of the tribes of the sons of Israel, [6]that this may be a sign among you, when your children ask in time to come, 'What do those stones mean to you?' [7]Then you shall tell them that the waters of the Jordan

---

3:4 two thousand cubits: About 1000 yards.

3:5 Sanctify yourselves: Perhaps involved washing garments and abstaining from sexual relations, as in Ex 19:14–15.

3:10 the living God: In contrast to the gods of the Gentiles, whose idols are speechless and powerless because they are lifeless (Ps 115:3–7; Hab 2:18–19; CCC 2112). **Canaanites ... Jebusites:** Seven of the ten nations that Israel had to conquer in order to take possession of the Promised Land (Gen 15:18–21). See note on Ex 3:8.

3:11 Lord of all the earth: The universal power and authority of Yahweh are in view (Deut 4:39). Israel's God is vastly superior to the deities of Canaan, whose influence was believed to be local rather than global.

3:15 the Jordan overflows: An annual spring event, when the melting snows of Mount Hermon cause downstream flooding. Stressing the high water level heightens the greatness of the miracle in 3:16–17. **time of harvest:** Begins in late March or early April.

3:16 Adam: A town roughly 18 miles upstream from the point of crossover. **the Salt Sea:** The Dead Sea, about six miles south of Jericho. **wholly cut off:** Stopping the flow of the Jordan is a miracle of divine power and providence. How the Lord effected the damming is not described, but

several reports in medieval and modern times attest to landslides, set off by seismic activity, that blocked the southward flow of the Jordan for up to one or two days. • *Allegorically,* the crossing of the Jordan is a type of Baptism. Just as the waters parted so that half drained down into the bitter sea, while the waters stopped upstream continued to be fresh, so some of the baptized return to the salty billows of sin, while others guard their sweetness and hold fast to the gift of God (Origen of Alexandria, *Homilies on Joshua* 4, 1–2).

4:1–24 Chapter 4 looks at the same event as chapter 3, only it fills in details of the Jordan crossing that were glossed over in the first narrative.

4:3 twelve stones: Represent the tribes of Israel that walk over the dry riverbed of the Jordan. These stones are carried to Gilgal and made into a lasting monument of the event (4:20–24). Another twelve stones are stacked up at the Jordan to mark the place where the Ark entered the waters (4:9). The author may intend a wordplay: the Hebrew for "stone" (*'eben*) closely resembles the word "son" (*ben*), reinforcing the link between the 12 stones and the 12 sons of Jacob, whose names are borne by the tribes. • *Allegorically,* the twelve stones set up at the Jordan are types of the twelve apostles acting as ministers of Baptism (St. Gregory of Nyssa, *On the Baptism of Jesus*).

4:7 memorial: Eight stone monuments are set up in Canaan, all bearing witness to the conquest of the land as well as the covenant between Yahweh and Israel (4:9, 20; 7:26; 8:29, 32; 10:27; 22:26–27; 24:27).

---

*3:7–17: The crossing of the Jordan is described in such a way as to bring out the theological parallelism with the crossing of the Red Sea (or, Sea of Reeds); both are seen as due to the direct intervention of God.

were cut off before the ark of the covenant of the LORD; when it passed over the Jordan, the waters of the Jordan were cut off. So these stones shall be to the sons of Israel a memorial for ever."

8 And the men of Israel did as Joshua commanded, and took up twelve stones out of the midst of the Jordan, according to the number of the tribes of the sons of Israel, as the LORD told Joshua; and they carried them over with them to the place where they lodged, and laid them down there. ⁹And Joshua set up twelve stones in the midst of the Jordan, in the place where the feet of the priests bearing the ark of the covenant had stood; and they are there to this day. ¹⁰For the priests who bore the ark stood in the midst of the Jordan, until everything was finished that the LORD commanded Joshua to tell the people, according to all that Moses had commanded Joshua.

The people passed over in haste; ¹¹and when all the people had finished passing over, the ark of the LORD and the priests passed over before the people. ¹²The sons of Reuben and the sons of Gad and the half-tribe of Manas'seh passed over armed before the sons of Israel, as Moses had bidden them; ¹³about forty thousand ready armed for war passed over before the LORD for battle, to the plains of Jericho. ¹⁴On that day the LORD exalted Joshua in the sight of all Israel; and they stood in awe of him, as they had stood in awe of Moses, all the days of his life.

15 And the LORD said to Joshua, ¹⁶"Command the priests who bear the ark of the covenant to come up out of the Jordan." ¹⁷Joshua therefore commanded the priests, "Come up out of the Jordan." ¹⁸And when the priests bearing the ark of the covenant of the LORD came up from the midst of the Jordan, and the soles of the priests' feet were lifted up on dry ground, the waters of the Jordan returned to their place and overflowed all its banks, as before.

19 The people came up out of the Jordan on the tenth day of the first month, and they encamped in Gilgal on the east border of Jericho. ²⁰And those twelve stones, which they took out of the Jordan, Joshua set up in Gilgal. ²¹And he said to the sons of Israel, "When your children ask their fathers in time to come, 'What do these stones mean?' ²²then you shall let your children know, 'Israel passed over this Jordan on dry ground.' ²³For the LORD your God dried up the waters of the Jordan for you until you passed over, as the LORD your God did to the Red Sea, which he dried up for us until we passed over, ²⁴so that all the peoples of the earth may know that the hand of the LORD is mighty; that you may fear the LORD your God for ever."

The Sons of Israel Are Circumcised

5 When all the kings of the Am'orites that were beyond the Jordan to the west, and all the kings of the Canaanites that were by the sea, heard that the LORD had dried up the waters of the Jordan for the sons of Israel until they had crossed over, their heart melted, and there was no longer any spirit in them, because of the sons of Israel.

2 At that time the LORD said to Joshua, "Make flint knives and circumcise the sons of Israel again the second time." ³So Joshua made flint knives, and circumcised the sons of Israel at Gib'eath-haar'aloth.ᵃ ⁴And this is the reason why Joshua circumcised them: all the males of the people who came out of Egypt, all the men of war, had died on the way in the wilderness after they had come out of Egypt. ⁵Though all the people who came out had been circumcised, yet all the people that were born on the way in the wilderness after they had come out of Egypt had not been circumcised. ⁶For the sons of Israel walked forty years in the wilderness, till all the nation, the men of war that came forth out

---

4:13 forty thousand: Fighting men from the Transjordan tribes of Reuben, Gad, and half-Manasseh. The full army of Israel is counted at 601,730 (Num 26:1–51). For a discussion of large numbers in the Bible, see note on Num 1:46.

4:19 first month: Abib, later called Nisan. It begins soon after the spring equinox in late March. The **tenth** of Abib is when the Israelites select lambs to be sacrificed on Passover (Ex 12:1–6). **Gilgal:** The name means "circle [of stones]". The site is located just inside the land of Canaan, northeast of Jericho. Gilgal serves as Joshua's base camp during the initial military phase of Israel's entrance into the land (10:7, 42–43; 14:6).

4:24 that all ... may know: Divine miracles are moments of divine revelation. News of the Lord's mighty acts makes his judgment (justice) and salvation (mercy) known even beyond the borders of Israel (2:10–11; 5:1; Ex 9:15–16; 15:13–16).

5:1–12 Israel's life in Canaan begins with two liturgical events: circumcision and Passover. Circumcision is the sign of the Abrahamic covenant (Gen 17:9–14) and the rite of initiation into the worshiping family of Israel (Lev 12:3). Passover commemorates the redemption from Egypt through a symbolic ritual meal (Ex 12:1–28). Service to the Lord readies Israel for the holy war that is about to ensue (chaps. 6–11).

5:1 Amorites: Occupy the central interior of Canaan. Amorites living east of the Jordan have already been conquered under Moses (Num 21:21–35). **Canaanites:** Concentrated in the western plains and coastlands of Canaan bordering the Mediterranean.

5:2 flint knives: Flint fractures into pieces with sharp edges. These can be used to make weapons and tools as well as surgical blades to perform circumcisions (Ex 4:25). **the second time:** Males born during the wilderness wandering enter Canaan uncircumcised (5:5). Blame for this negligence rests with their parents, the faithless Exodus generation (5:6). It is important to remedy this problem before Passover, since the paschal meal, which follows in 5:10, cannot be eaten by the uncircumcised (Ex 12:48). • *Allegorically,* Joshua, instead of Moses, leads a new people into Canaan to show that we enter the land of eternal life, not by the discipline of the Mosaic Law, but through the grace of a new law, being circumcised by the precepts of Jesus, whose name designates him a new Joshua (Tertullian, *Answer to the Jews* 9, 22). The second circumcision goes beyond the first, which is made in the flesh. It signifies the circumcision of the heart and spirit, something foretold by Moses and given by Christ, the true Joshua (Lactantius, *Divine Institutes* 4, 17).

5:6 perished: The demise of the Exodus generation was a divine punishment according to Num 13–14.

ᵃ That is *the hill of the foreskins.*

of Egypt, perished, because they did not listen to the voice of the Lord; to them the Lord swore that he would not let them see the land which the Lord had sworn to their fathers to give us, a land flowing with milk and honey. ⁷So it was their children, whom he raised up in their stead, that Joshua circumcised; for they were uncircumcised, because they had not been circumcised on the way.

8 When the circumcising of all the nation was done, they remained in their places in the camp till they were healed. ⁹And the Lord said to Joshua, "This day I have rolled away the reproach of Egypt from you." And so the name of that place is called Gilgalᵇ to this day.

The Passover at Gilgal

10 While the sons of Israel were encamped in Gilgal they kept the Passover on the fourteenth day of the month at evening in the plains of Jericho. ¹¹And on the next day after the Passover, on that very day, they ate of the produce of the land, unleavened cakes and parched grain. ¹²And the manna ceased on the next day, when they ate of the produce of the land; and the sons of Israel had manna no more, but ate of the fruit of the land of Canaan that year.

Joshua's Vision

13 When Joshua was by Jericho, he lifted up his eyes and looked, and behold, a man stood before him with his drawn sword in his hand; and Joshua went to him and said to him, "Are you for us, or for our adversaries?" ¹⁴And he said, "No; but as commander of the army of the Lord I have now come." And Joshua fell on his face to the earth, and worshiped, and said to him, "What does my lord bid his servant?" ¹⁵And the commander of the Lord's army said to Joshua, "Put off your shoes from your feet; for the place where you stand is holy." And Joshua did so.

Jericho Taken and Destroyed

6 *Now Jericho was shut up from within and from without because of the sons of Israel; none went out, and none came in. ²And the Lord said to Joshua, "See, I have given into your hand Jericho, with its king and mighty men of valor. ³You shall march around the city, all the men of war going around the city once. Thus shall you do for six days. ⁴And seven priests shall bear seven trumpets of rams' horns before the ark; and on the seventh day you shall march around the city seven times, the priests

---

5:9 reproach of Egypt: The events of the Exodus put Yahweh's reputation on the line. The mockery of Egypt was sure to come unless the Lord honored his promise (Ex 3:8) to establish Israel safely in the land (Ex 32:12; Num 14:13–16). **Gilgal:** By a play on words, the author associates Gilgal with the verb *galal*, meaning "to roll".

5:10 Passover: Paschal lambs are slaughtered on the fourteenth day of the first month and eaten after sundown (Ex 12:1–11). The last recorded observance of Passover was 39 years earlier, when Israel was still encamped at Sinai (Num 9:1–5).

5:12 the manna ceased: Yahweh fed Israel with this daily bread throughout the 40 years of wilderness wandering (Ex 16:35). Insofar as the manna tasted like wafers "made with honey" (Ex 16:31), it offered a foretaste of the Promised Land and its abundance of "milk and honey" (Ex 3:17). The end of the manna signals the beginning of a new era, when Israel reaps the blessings of Canaan. See note on Ex 16:4.

5:13 behold, a man: A warrior from heaven who speaks and acts on behalf of Yahweh. He appears to be the "angel of the Lord" who later departs from the camp at Gilgal and comes to Bochim (Judg 2:1–5). Joshua addresses him as "my lord" (5:14), showing that the battle plans for the Conquest are passed down the chain of command from heaven to earth. See word study: *Angel of the Lord* at Gen 16:7.

5:14 commander: The angel is to the hosts of heaven what Joshua is to the army of Israel: the leader of the Lord's fighting forces. His appearance indicates that the seizure of Canaan involves an unseen dimension of spiritual warfare.

5:15 where you stand is holy: Reminiscent of the holy ground at Sinai where Moses removed his sandals (Ex 3:5). For parallels between Joshua and Moses, see note on 1:5.

6:1–27 The conquest of Jericho. Yahweh is the lead character in the story: he orders the tactical strategy to be followed (6:2–5), he besieges the city by encircling it with the Ark (6:12–16), and he throws down the city's defenses, exposing it to attack (6:20). In these events, we see the Lord's *justice* in bringing judgment on the godless Canaanites, his *faithfulness* in fulfilling the Abrahamic promise to give Israel the land, and his *mercy* in protecting Rahab and her kin from destruction. • *Anagogically*, the fall of Jericho prefigures the end of the world. At the sound of God's trumpet, Jesus will come again to overthrow the world of wickedness, but he will save those like Rahab who received and obeyed the apostles he had sent (Origen of Alexandria, *Homilies on Joshua* 6, 4). The walls of Jericho are the frail defenses of this world, which will fall when God destroys death as the last enemy. Then only the one dwelling of the Church will be saved from the destruction of the ungodly (St. Augustine, *Against Faustus* 12, 31).

6:3 march around: The Jericho siege is as much a liturgical action as a military operation. Elements of worship and warfare are thus combined in several ways. **(1)** Both armed soldiers and vested priests make the circuit around the city (6:8–9). **(2)** The Ark of the Covenant, which is the focal point of Israel's worship as well as the Lord's battle chariot, is the centerpiece of the march (cf. 1 Chron 28:18). **(3)** Levitical priests blow trumpets that are used for liturgical as well as military purposes (Num 10:1–10). **(4)** The ceremony reaches a climax on the seventh day, the traditional day of rest that also became a day of sacrificial worship in Israel (Lev 23:3; Num 28:9–11). **(5)** The fiery destruction of Jericho may be likened to a sacrificial burnt offering, according to the theology of Deuteronomy (Dt 13:16).

6:4 seven: The number of trumpets, days, and processions around the city. Since in Hebrew the word seven (*sheba'*) shares the same root as the verb for swearing an oath (*shaba'*), the number may be featured prominently to signal the fulfillment of Yahweh's oath to grant Abraham's offspring the land of Canaan (Gen 15:18–21). • The second wave of judgments in the Book of Revelation comes with seven trumpets that result in the fall of the great city, Jerusalem, evoking memories of the fall of Jericho at the blast of seven trumpets (Rev 8:7—11:19). • Joshua appoints twelve to divide the inheritance of the land, and Jesus sent the twelve apostles into all the world. With a shout, the walls of Jericho come crashing down, and with the words of Jesus, "there will not be left here one stone upon another", the Jewish Temple lies fallen before our eyes (St. Cyril of Jerusalem, *Catechesis* 10, 11).

ᵇFrom Heb *galal* to roll.
*6:1: Here, as elsewhere, the history has been worked over in accordance with certain theological ideas.

blowing the trumpets. ⁵And when they make a long blast with the ram's horn, as soon as you hear the sound of the trumpet, then all the people shall shout with a great shout; and the wall of the city will fall down flat, and the people shall go up every man straight before him." ⁶So Joshua the son of Nun called the priests and said to them, "Take up the ark of the covenant, and let seven priests bear seven trumpets of rams' horns before the ark of the Lord." ⁷And he said to the people, "Go forward; march around the city, and let the armed men pass on before the ark of the Lord."

8 And as Joshua had commanded the people, the seven priests bearing the seven trumpets of rams' horns before the Lord went forward, blowing the trumpets, with the ark of the covenant of the Lord following them. ⁹And the armed men went before the priests who blew the trumpets, and the rear guard came after the ark, while the trumpets blew continually. ¹⁰But Joshua commanded the people, "You shall not shout or let your voice be heard, neither shall any word go out of your mouth, until the day I bid you shout; then you shall shout." ¹¹So he caused the ark of the Lord to compass the city, going about it once; and they came into the camp, and spent the night in the camp.

12 Then Joshua rose early in the morning, and the priests took up the ark of the Lord. ¹³And the seven priests bearing the seven trumpets of rams' horns before the ark of the Lord passed on, blowing the trumpets continually; and the armed men went

before them, and the rear guard came after the ark of the Lord, while the trumpets blew continually. ¹⁴And the second day they marched around the city once, and returned into the camp. So they did for six days.

15 On the seventh day they rose early at the dawn of day, and marched around the city in the same manner seven times: it was only on that day that they marched around the city seven times. ¹⁶And at the seventh time, when the priests had blown the trumpets, Joshua said to the people, "Shout; for the Lord has given you the city. ¹⁷And the city and all that is within it shall be devoted to the Lord for destruction;* only Ra'hab the harlot and all who are with her in her house shall live, because she hid the messengers that we sent. ¹⁸But you, keep yourselves from the things devoted to destruction, lest when you have devoted them you take any of the devoted things and make the camp of Israel a thing for destruction, and bring trouble upon it. ¹⁹But all silver and gold, and vessels of bronze and iron, are sacred to the Lord; they shall go into the treasury of the Lord." ²⁰So the people shouted, and the trumpets were blown. As soon as the people heard the sound of the trumpet, the people raised a great shout, and the wall fell down flat, so that the people went up into the city, every man straight before him, and they took the city. ²¹Then they utterly destroyed all in the city, both men and

(continued on p. 26)

6:19 the treasury: Located in the Tabernacle, called "the house of the Lord" in 6:24.

*6:17: Following the indications elsewhere in the Old Testament, it would appear that the ban, that is, the physical destruction of the enemy in obedience to the Deity, was practiced much less than a reading of Joshua might suggest. Despite the high religious principles that motivated it, it must be seen in the light of the imperfect stage of moral development reached at that time.

6:20 fell down flat: Literally, "fell down under it". Archaeological digs have revealed that Jericho's main defensive wall encircled the base of the mound, below street level for most of the city. Its mud brick fortifications collapsed outward rather than inward, an indication the walls were not rammed by a besieging army. Many scholars surmise that an earthquake toppled the fortifications. See note on 2:1–24. • According to the NT, it was the faith of Israel that moved God to slam down the walls of Jericho (Heb 11:30).

WORD STUDY

Devoted (6:17)

ḥerem (Heb.): means that something is "wholly dedicated" to Yahweh and so "banned" from profane use or personal possession. Devoted things can be persons or property given to the Lord by a vow (Lev 27:21, 28). The priests of the sanctuary are given charge over these donated items, which henceforth become the exclusive possession of God (Num 18:14). In the context of Israelite warfare, persons and things are dedicated to Yahweh by military destruction. So, for instance, when a city such as Jericho is placed under the *ḥerem* ban by God, all the inhabitants must be slain with the sword (Josh 6:17–21) and none of the spoils may be confiscated (Josh 7:1, 11; 1 Sam 15:21) without express permission from Yahweh (Josh 8:2, 27). Warriors who violate the ban on devoted things by taking what is forbidden place themselves under the law of devoted things and are set apart for ritual destruction (Josh 7:15; cf. Lev 27:29). A ban of utter destruction is placed on the cities of Canaan that are given to Israel as an inheritance (Deut 20:16–18) as well as on Israelite towns that forsake the Lord in favor of idols (Deut 13:15–17). Historically, the law of the ban is not restricted to Israel but is attested elsewhere in the Near East, most notably on the Moabite Stone of the ninth century B.C., which tells how King Mesha devoted a whole city to destruction in honor of the Moabite national god, Chemosh.

The Conquest of Canaan

Many people cringe when they read the war stories of the Book of Joshua. They wonder how the violence of the Conquest squares with the inspiration of the Bible and its faith in a loving and merciful God. The assault on Canaan goes far beyond Israel laying claim to a new homeland. Entire cities are burned and put to the sword, and neither soldier nor civilian is spared. The modern reader has every right to ask: What is the purpose behind this obliteration of human life? And what could possibly justify these extreme wartime tactics in the name of the Lord?

Questions such as these are by no means easy to answer. The Conquest narratives of Joshua are clearly among the "dark passages" of the Bible that Benedict XVI acknowledges are "obscure and difficult" (*Verbum Domini* 42). Nevertheless, we must make some effort to understand these stories within the framework of the Bible's message. However tempting it may be to sidestep the moral and theological dilemmas raised by these accounts, we do better to seek satisfying answers that will lead to a fuller understanding of God's revelation.

The testimony of Scripture coupled with the theological tradition of the Church offer several considerations that are relevant to the Conquest of Canaan and its purpose. No one of these points stands on its own as a complete explanation; nor do they compete with one another as alternative proposals. Instead, they are individual strands of evidence that may be drawn together into a reasonably coherent explanation for why Israel was authorized to seize control of Canaan by force of arms, even if some issues remain to be clarified.

Divine Judgment

At one level, the war on Canaan is a divine judgment on the "wickedness" of the Canaanites who lived there (Deut 9:4–5). When God first promised to give Abraham's descendants this land, he said they would have to wait until the "iniquity" of its inhabitants had reached its full measure (Gen 15:16). This period of waiting came to an end in the days of Moses and Joshua. Scripture underscores this fact when it documents the abominations of Canaanite culture. Religious worship in the land was thoroughly idolatrous, centered on a pantheon of gods and goddesses that included El, Baal, Asherah, Yam, Mot, and Molech, among others. Certain deities were venerated by a cult of child sacrifice (Lev 20:1–5; Deut 12:31), while shrines and sacred groves dedicated to others were places of gross sexual impurity (Hos 4:13–14). Incest, homosexuality, and bestiality reportedly flourished among the Canaanites (Lev 18:6–24), as did the practice of superstition and occultism (Deut 18:9–14). From the perspective of the Bible, then, the invasion of Canaan was a day of reckoning for a depraved and sacrilegious society (Wis 12:3–7).

Divine Protection

If the Conquest was an act of divine judgment on the Canaanites, it was also a form of divine protection for Israel. It is virtually certain that the sinful enticements of Canaanite culture, should they be allowed to thrive in the land, would quickly defile the purity of Israel's faith and life. Scripture draws attention to this spiritual aspect of the Conquest with its warnings against the dangers of idolatry for Israel (Ex 23:33; 34:11–16; Deut 7:4; 20:18). So, instead of leading Israel into the land and subjecting his people to a barrage of temptations and risks, Yahweh ordered the complete destruction of every trace of idolatry in Canaan (Num 33:50–53), including the idolaters who chose to fight rather than flee (Deut 7:1–5; 20:16–18). Drastic though it was, the offensive against Canaan was meant to ensure the spiritual welfare of God's people.

Divine Impartiality

Despite common misperceptions, the Conquest was not a form of ethnic cleansing aimed at exterminating a particular race of people. Its rationale was tied up with Canaan's evildoing, not its ethnicity. This is made clear in several ways. First, the scope of Israel's campaign is regional rather than racial. It was confined to the land that God was giving his people as an inheritance (Deut 20:16–18), a land occupied by at least ten different people groups (see Gen 15:18–21). Second, Canaanites such as Rahab and her family, having professed faith in Yahweh, were spared and welcomed into the covenant community (Josh 2:1–14; 6:23–25). Third, Scripture indicates that Israel was threatened by God with the same punitive action should it commit the same reprehensible crimes. Yahweh is the divine Owner of the land according to Lev 25:23; its inhabitants, regardless of their nationality or race, are no more than tenants and stewards. Consequently, the Israelites could expect to fare no better than the Canaanites should they defile the land with the same moral and religious debauchery. They too were faced with the possibility of forcible ejection from the land (Lev 18:28; Deut 28:63) and even a ban of utter destruction (Deut 4:25–26; Jer 25:9; Mal 4:6).

Divine Accommodation

It must be acknowledged that Israel's military mandate does not represent God's perfect plan for his people. Laws for making war on Canaanite settlements appear in Deuteronomy (Deut 20:1-20) among other legislation that was adapted to Israel's "hardness of heart" (Mt 19:8). These are among the laws that were "not good" (Ezek 20:25) because they represent a downward adjustment of God's higher standards for human conduct. The idea is that God lowered the bar of moral expectation in response to Israel's demonstrated weakness for idolatry. Several times after leaving Egypt, the people succumbed to the allurements of idol worship and sexual revelry (see Ex 32:1-6; Lev 17:7; Num 25:1-5). Having witnessed these failings, the Lord could hardly bring Israel into a land littered with idols and indecency without setting his people up for repeated acts of apostasy. One might even speculate that God wanted Israel to participate in his judgment on Canaan as a way of teaching the people at close range the horrible consequences of rejecting the covenant in favor of rank idolatry and immorality.

Divine Responsibility

Perhaps the most disturbing aspect of the Conquest is the killing of non-combatants such as women and children (Deut 2:34; 3:6; Josh 6:21). At least in the case of infants and children, we cannot speak of all the Canaanites being guilty of punishable crimes. That said, the Bible is emphatic that God is the Lord of life and death (Deut 32:39; 1 Sam 2:6). It is fully within the scope of his sovereign authority to determine "when" and "under what circumstances" the life of his creatures begins and ends. It is true that the Lord takes no delight in the death of the living (Ezek 18:32; Wis 1:13), and yet the fact remains that death comes to everyone as a consequence of sin (Gen 3:19; Rom 5:12). Death that results from violence or external force can be evaluated differently in different circumstances. It is unjustified and gravely sinful when one person takes the life of another without the authority to do so. This is forbidden as murder (Ex 20:13; Deut 5:17). But under strictly limited conditions, it can be justified for civil authorities to take lethal action against a society's most dangerous criminals. Hence, the Bible recognizes the legitimacy of capital punishment (Ex 21:12-17; Rom 13:7). Human agents can thus be charged with administering a death sentence, but they are not thereby murderers, since they act on the orders of a legitimate authority. The same can be said for the angels, who are likewise moral beings. When God sent "destroying angels" (Ps 78:49) to slay the firstborn of Egypt (Ex 12:23-27), the angels administered the plague with impunity, since they acted on the authority of God, who alone is responsible for smiting the Egyptians (Ex 12:29). The Conquest of Canaan is analogous to these situations. The people of Israel, in wielding the sword of war, act on God's authority as an instrument and executor of divine judgment. This is one way that Catholic theologians have explained the assault on Canaan (St. Augustine, *City of God* 1, 21; St. Thomas Aquinas, *Summa Theologiae* I-II, 105, 3).

Divine Pedagogy

Ultimately the "dark passages" of the Old Testament must be viewed in the light of Christ and the New Testament. From this perspective, the historical character of divine revelation is of paramount importance. God did not disclose the fullness of his saving truth all at once. Rather, he led Israel by stages through a process of moral and spiritual education that only gradually lifted them out of the darkness of less civilized times. This has been compared to raising a child from infancy to adulthood (St. Augustine, *City of God* 10, 14). Instruction is simple at first, and much that is imperfect and immature is tolerated at various stages along the way. Hence, we should not expect to find the fullness of Christian morality or theology operative in pre-Christian times any more than second graders should be expected to know calculus or make decisions about college. Only when the pedagogical process is complete do we arrive at the intended goal. The warfare laws of Deuteronomy stand at an early stage of Israel's formation, at a time when the danger of idolatry was the overriding concern. The moral standards revealed by Jesus, which bid us to love our enemies and to do them good, were still many centuries away (Mt 5:44). Likewise, the gospel reveals that this life is only a prelude to eternal life, where God's perfect justice will right the wrongs of history. How do the ancient Canaanites—especially their young ones— fit into this picture? Only God knows for certain. Still, we can be confident that Christ, the innocent Sufferer par excellence, will show his mercy beyond what any deserves. In this way, we can interpret Scripture's most difficult texts in a way that "enables their meaning to emerge in the light of the mystery of Christ" (Benedict XVI, *Verbum Domini* 42).

women, young and old, oxen, sheep, and donkeys, with the edge of the sword.

22 And Joshua said to the two men who had spied out the land, "Go into the harlot's house, and bring out from it the woman, and all who belong to her, as you swore to her." [23]So the young men who had been spies went in, and brought out Ra'hab, and her father and mother and brothers and all who belonged to her; and they brought all her kindred, and set them outside the camp of Israel. [24]And they burned the city with fire, and all within it; only the silver and gold, and the vessels of bronze and of iron, they put into the treasury of the house of the LORD. [25]But Ra'hab the harlot, and her father's household, and all who belonged to her, Joshua saved alive; and she dwelt in Israel to this day, because she hid the messengers whom Joshua sent to spy out Jericho.

26 Joshua laid an oath upon them at that time, saying, "Cursed before the LORD be the man that rises up and rebuilds this city, Jericho.

At the cost of his first-born shall he lay its
   foundation,
   and at the cost of his youngest son shall he set up
   its gates."

27 So the LORD was with Joshua; and his fame was in all the land.

The Sin of Achan and Its Punishment

7 But the sons of Israel broke faith in regard to the devoted things; for A'chan the son of Carmi, son of Zabdi, son of Ze'rah, of the tribe of Judah, took some of the devoted things; and the anger of the LORD burned against the sons of Israel.

2 Joshua sent men from Jericho to Ai, which is near Beth-a'ven, east of Bethel, and said to them, "Go up and spy out the land." And the men went up and spied out Ai. [3]And they returned to Joshua, and said to him, "Let not all the people go up, but let about two or three thousand men go up and attack Ai; do not make the whole people toil up there, for they are but few." [4]So about three thousand went

up there from the people; and they fled before the men of Ai, [5]and the men of Ai killed about thirty-six men of them, and chased them before the gate as far as Sheb'arim, and slew them at the descent. And the hearts of the people melted, and became as water.

6 Then Joshua tore his clothes, and fell to the earth upon his face before the ark of the LORD until the evening, he and the elders of Israel; and they put dust upon their heads. [7]And Joshua said, "Alas, O Lord GOD, why have you brought this people over the Jordan at all, to give us into the hands of the Am'orites, to destroy us? Would that we had been content to dwell beyond the Jordan! [8]O Lord, what can I say, when Israel has turned their backs before their enemies! [9]For the Canaanites and all the inhabitants of the land will hear of it, and will surround us, and cut off our name from the earth; and what will you do for your great name?"

10 The LORD said to Joshua, "Arise, why have you thus fallen upon your face? [11]Israel has sinned; they have transgressed my covenant which I commanded them; they have taken some of the devoted things; they have stolen, and lied, and put them among their own stuff. [12]Therefore the sons of Israel cannot stand before their enemies; they turn their backs before their enemies, because they have become a thing for destruction. I will be with you no more, unless you destroy the devoted things from among you. [13]Up, sanctify the people, and say, 'Sanctify yourselves for tomorrow; for thus says the LORD, God of Israel, "There are devoted things in the midst of you, O Israel; you cannot stand before your enemies, until you take away the devoted things from among you." [14]In the morning therefore you shall be brought near by your tribes; and the tribe which the LORD takes shall come near by families; and the family which the LORD takes shall come near by households; and the household which the LORD takes shall come near man by man. [15]And

---

6:26: 1 Kings 16:34.

6:25 Rahab ... in Israel: She eventually married a man of Judah, named Salmon, and became an ancestor of King David (Ruth 4:21; Mt 1:5). See note on 2:1.

7:1 Israel broke faith: By stealing property consecrated to Yahweh. The culprit is revealed to be **Achan**, who took spoils from Jericho and hid them in his tent (7:21). His thievery was a double violation of the military ban: **(1)** he confiscated a mantle instead of destroying it, as stipulated in 6:17, and **(2)** he smuggled out silver and gold that should have gone to the Lord's treasury, as stipulated in 6:19. On the ban, see word study: *Devoted* at 6:17.

7:2 Ai: Means "ruin" or possibly "stone heap". The town was west of Jericho, close to Bethel (12:9). Archaeology has long located Ai at the site of Khirbet et-Tell, but the identification is problematic, not least because excavations suggest a long gap in occupation between ca. 2400 and 1200 B.C. An alternative case has been made for locating Ai elsewhere at Khirbet Nisya. **Beth-aven:** A shrine near Bethel or, possibly, a derogatory epithet (meaning "house of evil") for Bethel itself (cf. Hos 4:15; 10:5).

7:5 hearts ... melted: Fear grips the people of Israel as it had the Canaanites who heard of their coming (2:11; 5:1).

7:6 tore his clothes: A sign of extreme distress (Gen 37:34; Judg 11:35).

7:7 why: A cry of faith struggling with frustration. Joshua wrestles with the defeat at Ai and wonders aloud how this humiliating setback fits with God's promise to give Israel the land. Moses voiced a similar prayer when the Lord's promise of deliverance seemed lost in the pain of a worsening situation (Ex 5:22-23).

7:11 Israel has sinned: The statement implies two things. **(1)** Sin blocks the success of Israel in taking possession of the land. Here, the retreat from Ai is the tragic result of Achan's secret violation of the military ban back at Jericho. **(2)** The community of Israel is bound together in moral solidarity, so that any one violation of the ban triggers a ban of destruction on Israel as a whole (see 6:18).

he who is taken with the devoted things shall be burned with fire, he and all that he has, because he has transgressed the covenant of the LORD, and because he has done a shameful thing in Israel.'"

16 So Joshua rose early in the morning, and brought Israel near tribe by tribe, and the tribe of Judah was taken; ¹⁷and he brought near the families of Judah, and the family of the Ze′rahites was taken; and he brought near the family of the Zerahites man by man, and Zabdi was taken; ¹⁸and he brought near his household man by man, and A′chan the son of Carmi, son of Zabdi, son of Ze′rah of the tribe of Judah, was taken. ¹⁹Then Joshua said to A′chan, "My son, give glory to the LORD God of Israel, and render praise to him; and tell me now what you have done; do not hide it from me." ²⁰And A′chan answered Joshua, "Of a truth I have sinned against the LORD God of Israel, and this is what I did: ²¹when I saw among the spoil a beautiful mantle from Shi′nar, and two hundred shekels of silver, and a bar of gold weighing fifty shekels, then I coveted them, and took them; and behold, they are hidden in the earth inside my tent, with the silver underneath."

22 So Joshua sent messengers, and they ran to the tent; and behold, it was hidden in his tent with the silver underneath. ²³And they took them out of the tent and brought them to Joshua and all the sons of Israel; and they laid them down before the LORD. ²⁴And Joshua and all Israel with him took A′chan the son of Ze′rah, and the silver and the mantle and the bar of gold, and his sons and daughters, and his oxen and donkeys and sheep, and his tent, and all that he had; and they brought them up to the Valley of A′chor. ²⁵And Joshua said, "Why did you bring trouble on us? The LORD brings trouble on you today." And all Israel stoned him with stones; they burned them with fire, and stoned them with stones. ²⁶And they raised over him a great heap of stones that remains to this day; then the LORD turned from his burning anger. Therefore to this day the name of that place is called the Valley of A′chor.ᶜ

Capture and Destruction of Ai

8 And the LORD said to Joshua, "Do not fear or be dismayed; take all the fighting men with you, and arise, go up to Ai; see, I have given into your hand the king of Ai, and his people, his city, and his land; ²and you shall do to Ai and its king as you did to Jericho and its king; only its spoil and its cattle you shall take as booty for yourselves; lay an ambush against the city, behind it."

3 So Joshua arose, and all the fighting men, to go up to Ai; and Joshua chose thirty thousand mighty men of valor, and sent them forth by night. ⁴And he commanded them, "Behold, you shall lie in ambush against the city, behind it; do not go very far from the city, but hold yourselves all in readiness; ⁵and I, and all the people who are with me, will approach the city. And when they come out against us, as before, we shall flee before them; ⁶and they will come out after us, till we have drawn them away from the city; for they will say, 'They are fleeing from us, as before.' So we will flee from them; ⁷then you shall rise up from the ambush, and seize the city; for the LORD your God will give it into your hand. ⁸And when you have taken the city, you shall

---

7:16 was taken: Probably by casting lots, just as the tribal territories were assigned (14:2). The Lord works through this procedure of selection and elimination to point the finger of blame at Achan (7:18).

7:19 give glory to the LORD: A juridical formula that puts Achan under oath to speak the truth (Jn 9:24).

7:21 saw ... coveted ... took: Reminiscent of Gen 3:6, where Eve sees, desires, and takes the forbidden fruit. Death by divine judgment is the tragic result in both cases (7:25; Gen 2:17; 3:19).

7:25 stoned them: The execution of Achan and his household. It is difficult to understand why the family of the criminal shares the fate of the criminal himself. A few considerations may be noted. **(1)** Some scholars maintain that the Hebrew MT of this verse is partially corrupt due to tampering by later scribes. The Greek LXX, by contrast, states that Israel stoned "him" (= Achan) but says nothing about the killing of his family. **(2)** It may be that Achan's family knew of his crime and agreed to keep it secret or at least made no attempt to expose it. Either way, their inaction would make them guilty accomplices to a transgression that endangered the entire covenant community (6:18). **(3)** In ancient Israel the family was considered a corporate unity in which the merits or demerits of one member could bring corresponding consequences upon all. We witness this principle at work in Joshua: just as Rahab, by her submission, wins mercy and deliverance for her entire family (6:23), so Achan, by his sin, brings judgment on his entire household (7:25; cf. Ex 20:5).

7:26 heap of stones: Achan's body is buried under a pile of rocks, the same treatment given to the enemies of Israel (8:29; 10:27). This crude memorial stands as a warning to others against violating the covenant. **the Valley of Achor:** Named in remembrance of the "trouble" that Achan brings upon the people (7:25). The toponym likewise resembles the name "Achan", which is spelled "Achar" in 1 Chron 2:7 and throughout the Greek LXX. • The prophet Hosea, looking to a future age, envisions the Valley of Achor as one day becoming a sign of hope.

8:1–29 The conquest of Ai. Employing a classic military tactic of diversion and ambush, the city is sacked from the west after its defenders charge out after warriors fleeing east. The king of Ai is then captured (8:23), all servicemen and civilians are killed (8:24), and the city is set ablaze (8:19, 28). On the location of Ai, see note on 7:2.

8:2 take as booty: An exemption from the law of total destruction for Canaanite cities as stated in Deut 20:16–18. Although Ai and its inhabitants would normally fall under the ban on wartime spoils, on this occasion their livestock and possessions could be plundered for Israelite use (8:27). Following the Achan incident in chapter 7, where taking spoils resulted in defeat and death, the relaxation of the ban for Ai appears to be an instance of divine accommodation, i.e., an example of God lowering the bar of moral expectation because of his people's weakness of will. On the ban, see word study: *Devoted* at 6:17.

ᶜThat is *Trouble.*

set the city on fire, doing as the Lord has bidden; see, I have commanded you." ⁹So Joshua sent them forth; and they went to the place of ambush, and lay between Bethel and Ai, to the west of Ai; but Joshua spent that night among the people.

10 And Joshua arose early in the morning and mustered the people, and went up, with the elders of Israel, before the people to Ai. ¹¹And all the fighting men who were with him went up, and drew near before the city, and encamped on the north side of Ai, with a ravine between them and Ai. ¹²And he took about five thousand men, and set them in ambush between Bethel and Ai, to the west of the city. ¹³So they stationed the forces, the main encampment which was north of the city and its rear guard west of the city. But Joshua spent that night in the valley. ¹⁴And when the king of Ai saw this he and all his people, the men of the city, made haste and went out early to the descent ᵈ toward the Arabah to meet Israel in battle; but he did not know that there was an ambush against him behind the city. ¹⁵And Joshua and all Israel made a pretense of being beaten before them, and fled in the direction of the wilderness. ¹⁶So all the people who were in the city were called together to pursue them, and as they pursued Joshua they were drawn away from the city. ¹⁷There was not a man left in Ai or Bethel, who did not go out after Israel; they left the city open, and pursued Israel.

18 Then the Lord said to Joshua, "Stretch out the javelin that is in your hand toward Ai; for I will give it into your hand." And Joshua stretched out the javelin that was in his hand toward the city. ¹⁹And the ambush rose quickly out of their place, and as soon as he had stretched out his hand, they ran and entered the city and took it; and they made haste to set the city on fire. ²⁰So when the men of Ai looked back, behold, the smoke of the city went up

to heaven; and they had no power to flee this way or that, for the people that fled to the wilderness turned back upon the pursuers. ²¹And when Joshua and all Israel saw that the ambush had taken the city, and that the smoke of the city went up, then they turned back and struck the men of Ai. ²²And the others came forth from the city against them; so they were in the midst of Israel, some on this side, and some on that side; and Israel struck them, until there was left none that survived or escaped. ²³But the king of Ai they took alive, and brought him to Joshua.

24 When Israel had finished slaughtering all the inhabitants of Ai in the open wilderness where they pursued them, and all of them to the very last had fallen by the edge of the sword, all Israel returned to Ai, and struck it with the edge of the sword. ²⁵And all who fell that day, both men and women, were twelve thousand, all the people of Ai. ²⁶For Joshua did not draw back his hand, with which he stretched out the javelin, until he had utterly destroyed all the inhabitants of Ai. ²⁷Only the cattle and the spoil of that city Israel took as their booty, according to the word of the Lord which he commanded Joshua. ²⁸So Joshua burned Ai, and made it for ever a heap of ruins, as it is to this day. ²⁹And he hanged the king of Ai on a tree until evening; and at the going down of the sun Joshua commanded, and they took his body down from the tree, and cast it at the entrance of the gate of the city, and raised over it a great heap of stones, which stands there to this day.

Joshua Sacrifices and Reads the Law at Mount Ebal

30 Then Joshua built an altar on Mount E'bal to the Lord, the God of Israel, ³¹as Moses the servant of the Lord had commanded the sons of Israel, as it is written in the book of the law of Moses, "an altar

---

8:30–35: Deut 27:2–8.

8:12 five thousand men: It is uncertain how this division of 5,000 soldiers selected for the ambush relates to the 30,000 men chosen for this purpose in 8:3. Perhaps two divisions were placed in two strategic positions, both to the west of the city.

8:15 direction of the wilderness: East of Ai.

8:17 Bethel: Joins nearby Ai in the fight against Israel (12:9). Archaeology has long located Bethel at modern Beitin, although an alternative case has been made for the site of Bireh, which more closely matches the biblical data. The kings of Bethel and Ai are both slain in this attack (8:29; 12:16).

8:18 stretched out the javelin: More than a battlefield signal to trigger the ambush. Joshua keeps his arm extended throughout the day's battle (8:26), much as Moses kept his arms stretched out in prayer while Israel triumphed over the Amalekites at the start of the Exodus (Ex 17:11–13). For other parallels between Joshua and Moses, see note on 1:5.

8:28 Joshua burned Ai: Only two other cities were destroyed with fire during the initial phase of the conquest: Jericho (6:24) and Hazor (11:11).

8:29 hanged the king: First the king is executed, and then his corpse is impaled (or otherwise fixed) to a tree. This gruesome display of the king's lifeless body is a sign that God has smitten him with a curse (Deut 21:22–23).

8:30–35 The public ratification of the Deuteronomic covenant as prescribed by Moses in Deut 27:1–26. The priests conduct the sacrificial liturgy, while the lay tribes participate by swearing oaths to keep the terms of the covenant expressed in the laws of Deuteronomy. The ceremony takes place at Shechem, a city in central Palestine seated between Mount Ebal (north) and Mount Gerizim (south). • The location is significant, for Shechem is the place where Yahweh first promised to give the land of Canaan to Abraham's descendants and where Abraham first raised an altar in honor of the Lord (Gen 12:6–8).

8:31 unhewn stones: Piled up to form a rough mound rather than tooled by masons and stacked into a squared platform. The hewing restriction comes from Deut 27:5 but is also in line with Ex 20:25.

ᵈCn: Heb *appointed time.*

of unhewn stones, upon which no man has lifted an iron tool"; and they offered on it burnt offerings to the LORD, and sacrificed peace offerings. ³²And there, in the presence of the sons of Israel, he wrote upon the stones a copy of the law of Moses, which he had written. ³³And all Israel, sojourner as well as homeborn, with their elders and officers and their judges, stood on opposite sides of the ark before the Levitical priests who carried the ark of the covenant of the LORD, half of them in front of Mount Ger'izim and half of them in front of Mount E'bal, as Moses the servant of the LORD had commanded at the first, that they should bless the sons of Israel. ³⁴And afterward he read all the words of the law, the blessing and the curse, according to all that is written in the book of the law. ³⁵There was not a word of all that Moses commanded which Joshua did not read before all the assembly of Israel, and the women, and the little ones, and the sojourners who lived among them.

The Gibeonites' Stratagem

9 When all the kings who were beyond the Jordan in the hill country and in the lowland all along the coast of the Great Sea toward Lebanon, the Hittites, the Am'orites, the Canaanites, the Per'izzites, the Hi'vites, and the Jeb'usites, heard of this, ²they gathered together with one accord to fight Joshua and Israel.

3 But when the inhabitants of Gib'eon heard what Joshua had done to Jericho and to Ai, ⁴they on their part acted with cunning, and went and made ready provisions, and took worn-out sacks upon their donkeys, and wineskins, worn-out and torn and mended, ⁵with worn-out, patched sandals on their feet, and worn-out clothes; and all their provisions were dry and moldy. ⁶And they went to Joshua

---

8:33 bless the sons of Israel: A priestly action (Lev 9:22; Num 6:22–27).

9:1–2 Local Canaanites forge a military alliance to resist and repel Israel's advance through the land. The coalition will prove futile, however, since God has sworn to drive them out and to give their territory to his chosen people (Gen 15:18–21).

9:3 Gibeon: Several miles southwest of Ai, securely located at modern el-Jib. The residents of Gibeon are not the foreign travelers they pretend to be (9:6) but are "Hivites" (9:7) long settled in the land of Canaan (9:1).

CONQUEST OF CENTRAL AND SOUTHERN CANAAN (JOSHUA 3–10)

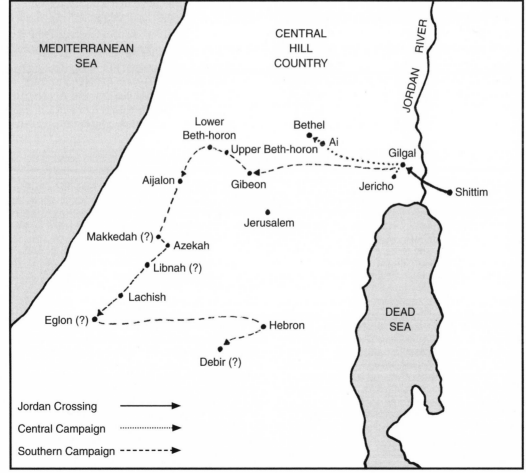

in the camp at Gilgal, and said to him and to the men of Israel, "We have come from a far country; so now make a covenant with us." ⁷But the men of Israel said to the Hi′vites, "Perhaps you live among us; then how can we make a covenant with you?" ⁸They said to Joshua, "We are your servants." And Joshua said to them, "Who are you? And where do you come from?" ⁹They said to him, "From a very far country your servants have come, because of the name of the LORD your God; for we have heard a report of him, and all that he did in Egypt, ¹⁰and all that he did to the two kings of the Am′orites who were beyond the Jordan, Si′hon the king of Heshbon, and Og king of Bashan, who dwelt in Ash′taroth. ¹¹And our elders and all the inhabitants of our country said to us, 'Take provisions in your hand for the journey, and go to meet them, and say to them, "We are your servants; come now, make a covenant with us."' ¹²Here is our bread; it was still warm when we took it from our houses as our food for the journey, on the day we set forth to come to you, but now, behold, it is dry and moldy; ¹³these wineskins were new when we filled them, and behold, they are burst; and these garments and shoes of ours are worn out from the very long journey." ¹⁴So the men partook of their provisions, and did not ask direction from the LORD. ¹⁵And Joshua made peace with them, and made a covenant with them, to let them live; and the leaders of the congregation swore to them.

16 At the end of three days after they had made a covenant with them, they heard that they were their neighbors, and that they dwelt among them. ¹⁷And the sons of Israel set out and reached their cities on the third day. Now their cities were Gib′eon, Chephi′rah, Be-er′oth, and Kir′iath-je′arim. ¹⁸But the sons of Israel did not kill them, because the leaders of the congregation had sworn to them by the LORD, the God of Israel. Then all the congregation murmured against the leaders. ¹⁹But all the leaders said to all the congregation, "We have sworn to them by the LORD, the God of Israel, and now we may not touch them. ²⁰This we will do to them, and let them live, lest wrath be upon us, because of the oath which we swore to them." ²¹And the leaders said to them, "Let them live." So they became hewers of wood and drawers of water for all the congregation, as the leaders had said of them.

22 Joshua summoned them, and he said to them, "Why did you deceive us, saying, 'We are very far from you,' when you dwell among us? ²³Now therefore you are cursed, and some of you shall always be slaves, hewers of wood and drawers of water for the house of my God." ²⁴They answered Joshua, "Because it was told to your servants for a certainty that the LORD your God had commanded his servant Moses to give you all the land, and to destroy all the inhabitants of the land from before you; so we feared greatly for our lives because of you, and did this thing. ²⁵And now, behold, we are in your hand: do as it seems good and right in your sight to do to us." ²⁶So he did to them, and delivered them out of the hand of the sons of Israel; and they did not kill them. ²⁷But Joshua made them that day hewers of wood and drawers of water for the congregation and for the altar of the LORD, to continue to this day, in the place which he should choose.

The Sun Stands Still

10 When Ado′ni-ze′dek king of Jerusalem heard how Joshua had taken Ai, and had utterly destroyed it, doing to Ai and its king as he had done to Jericho and its king, and how the inhabitants of Gib′eon had made peace with Israel and were among them, ²he* feared greatly, because Gib′eon was a great city, like one of the royal cities, and because it was greater than Ai, and all its men were mighty. ³So Ado′ni-ze′dek king of Jerusalem sent to

---

9:10 Sihon … Og: Former kings whose territory was conquered by Israel on the eve of the Conquest (Num 21:21–35).

9:14 did not ask direction: Failure to discern the Lord's will leads to a foolish mistake. For in the very act of *making* a covenant with the Gibeonites, the people of Israel are *breaking* their covenant with God, who forbade treaties and alliances with the indigenous peoples of Canaan (Ex 23:32; 34:12; Deut 7:2). Instead of rushing through negotiations, Israel should have consulted Yahweh, who alone could see beyond the frayed clothing to the heart of the Gibeonite deception.

9:15 made peace: Israel ratifies a covenant of nonaggression with Gibeon by sworn oaths and shared food (cf. Gen 31:44–54). The treaty obligates Israel, the superior partner, to protect the life of the Gibeonites (10:6) under a threat of divine curses (9:20). The binding force of this covenant will become apparent in later biblical history when a famine ravages the land of Israel because Saul has violated the covenant by putting some of the Gibeonites to death (2 Sam 21:1–9). **made a covenant:** Literally "cut a covenant", alluding to an ancient cursing ritual that involved slaying an animal as part of the ratification ceremony.

9:21 hewers … drawers: The Gibeonites will serve both the people and sanctuary of Israel as woodcutters and water carriers (9:23, 27). Supplies of wood were needed for the fires of the Tabernacle altar, and water was needed for ritual washings. Solomon later makes the remnant of the Canaanites into slave laborers for his building projects (1 Kings 9:20–21).

9:27 the place: I.e., the place of Israelite worship to be chosen by Yahweh (Deut 12:10–14). The sanctuary was stationed in Shiloh in Joshua's day (18:1); later, Jerusalem was selected as the place of the Lord's holy dwelling (1 Kings 9:1–3).

10:1–43 The southern campaign. Joshua routs a coalition of five Canaanite city-states and raids multiple fortified towns south of Jerusalem. Coupled with the overthrow of Jericho, Ai, and Bethel, as well as the subjugation of Gibeon, these military expeditions bring key areas of central and southern Canaan under Israelite control. Nevertheless, several towns and territories in the region remain to be conquered by future generations (13:1–4; Judg 1:1–21). Note that Israel's offensive campaigns in chaps. 6–9 switches to defensive warfare in chaps. 10–11.

10:1 Jerusalem: Formerly called "Salem" (Gen 14:18; Ps 76:2). It was also known in early times as Jebus (18:28), since the city was a Jebusite stronghold (15:63) before David made it the capital of Israel (2 Sam 5:6–9).

ˣHeb *they.*

Hoham king of He'bron, to Piram king of Jarmuth, to Japhi'a king of La'chish, and to De'bir king of Eg'lon, saying, ⁴"Come up to me, and help me, and let us strike Gib'eon; for it has made peace with Joshua and with the sons of Israel." ⁵Then the five kings of the Am'orites, the king of Jerusalem, the king of He'bron, the king of Jarmuth, the king of La'chish, and the king of Eg'lon, gathered their forces, and went up with all their armies and encamped against Gib'eon, and made war against it.

6 And the men of Gib'eon sent to Joshua at the camp in Gilgal, saying, "Do not relax your hand from your servants; come up to us quickly, and save us, and help us; for all the kings of the Am'orites that dwell in the hill country are gathered against us." ⁷So Joshua went up from Gilgal, he and all the people of war with him, and all the mighty men of valor. ⁸And the LORD said to Joshua, "Do not fear them, for I have given them into your hands; there shall not a man of them stand before you." ⁹So Joshua came upon them suddenly, having marched up all night from Gilgal. ¹⁰And the LORD threw them into a panic before Israel, who slew them with a great slaughter at Gib'eon, and chased them by the way of the ascent of Beth-ho'ron, and struck them as far as Aze'kah and Makke'dah. ¹¹And as they fled before Israel, while they were going down the ascent of Beth-ho'ron, the LORD threw down great stones from heaven upon them as far as Aze'kah, and they died; there were more who died because of the hailstones than the men of Israel killed with the sword.

12 Then spoke Joshua to the LORD in the day when the LORD gave the Am'orites over to the men of Israel; and he said in the sight of Israel,

"Sun, stand still at Gib'eon,
and you Moon in the valley of Ai'jalon."
¹³And the sun stood still, and the moon stayed,
until the nation took vengeance on their enemies.
Is this not written in the Book of Jash'ar? The sun stayed in the midst of heaven, and did not hasten to go down for about a whole day. ¹⁴There has been no day like it before or since, when the LORD listened to the voice of a man; for the LORD fought for Israel.*

15 Then Joshua returned, and all Israel with him, to the camp at Gilgal.

Five Kings Defeated

16 These five kings fled, and hid themselves in the cave at Makke'dah. ¹⁷And it was told Joshua, "The five kings have been found, hidden in the cave at Makke'dah." ¹⁸And Joshua said, "Roll great stones against the mouth of the cave, and set men by it to guard them; ¹⁹but do not stay there yourselves, pursue your enemies, fall upon their rear, do not let them enter their cities; for the LORD your God has given them into your hand." ²⁰When Joshua and the men of Israel had finished slaying them with a very great slaughter, until they were wiped out, and when the remnant which remained of them had entered into the fortified cities, ²¹all the people returned safe to Joshua in the camp at Makke'dah; not a man moved his tongue against any of the sons of Israel.

22 Then Joshua said, "Open the mouth of the cave, and bring those five kings out to me from the cave." ²³And they did so, and brought those five kings out to him from the cave, the king of Jerusalem, the king of He'bron, the king of Jarmuth, the king of La'chish, and the king of Eg'lon. ²⁴And when they brought those kings out to Joshua,

---

10:6 save us: The peace treaty made in 9:15 obligates Israel to aid and defend its Gibeonite vassals from hostile aggression. The appeal for help made to Joshua is an appeal for him to honor this covenant responsibility.

10:9 marched up: It is a strenuous uphill climb of nearly 20 miles from Gilgal in the Jordan valley to Gibeon in the central highlands.

10:10 Beth-horon: Near a northwest escape route that leads out of the hill country down to the coastal plain. **Azekah and Makkedah:** Cities southwest of Gibeon. The exact location of the latter is uncertain.

10:11 stones from heaven: Yahweh pounds the coalition fighters with a violent hailstorm. Here and elsewhere God is the divine Warrior who wields the weapons of nature to strike down the enemies of Israel with deadly force (Ex 9:23–25; Job 38:22–23; Wis 5:17–23).

10:13 the sun stood still: Joshua's prayer calls forth an unforgettable miracle, the exact nature of which is disputed. The crucial question is whether the poetic fragment should be understood literally or figuratively. **(1)** Taken *literally*, the poem can be said to describe a "cosmic" miracle, whereby the Lord halts the sun in its course by stopping the rotation of the earth for an entire day. This reading of the verse must take account of the prescientific viewpoint of the ancient author, whose sense experience would suggest that the sun is in motion rather than the earth. **(2)** Taken *figuratively*, the poem may be said to celebrate a "military" miracle, whereby God enables the army of Israel to accomplish the work of two days in one day's time. On this reading, the day of battle seems to be amazingly prolonged because Joshua and his men win a complete victory and accomplish all of their military objectives before sunset. Whether the miracle is in the sky or on the ground, the event can only be explained as Yahweh's supernatural intervention on behalf of Israel. **Book of Jashar:** A lost collection of epic Hebrew poetry. The work is known only from two excerpts, one in Josh 10:12–13 and another in 2 Sam 1:18–27.

10:14 voice of a man: The miracle at Gibeon illustrates not only the power of God but also the power of prayer. Here it is the plea of righteous Joshua that moves heaven into action on behalf of the covenant people (10:12; Jas 5:16).

10:24 feet upon the necks: A victory stance, the foot of the conqueror pressing down on the head and neck of the defeated foe. Depictions of this wartime ritual can be seen in the royal artwork of Egypt and Assyria. The biblical expression "under the feet" is linked to this ancient custom (1 Kings 5:3; Ps 110:1; 1 Cor 15:25–28; Ps 66:12).

---

*10:12–14: Joshua's apostrophe to the sun occurs in a fragment quoted from an old collection of epic material, and the quotation goes on beyond verse 12. This would make a literal interpretation of this event undesirable. It appears from the narrative that a great storm occurred at the same time as the attack and powerfully helped toward the Israelite victory (verse 11). It is this sign of divine aid that is so graphically apostrophized in the following poetic fragment (verses 12–13).

Joshua summoned all the men of Israel, and said to the chiefs of the men of war who had gone with him, "Come near, put your feet upon the necks of these kings." Then they came near, and put their feet on their necks. 25And Joshua said to them, "Do not be afraid or dismayed; be strong and of good courage; for thus the LORD will do to all your enemies against whom you fight." 26And afterward Joshua struck them and put them to death, and he hung them on five trees. And they hung upon the trees until evening; 27but at the time of the going down of the sun, Joshua commanded, and they took them down from the trees, and threw them into the cave where they had hidden themselves, and they set great stones against the mouth of the cave, which remain to this very day.

28 And Joshua took Makke'-dah on that day, and struck it and its king with the edge of the sword; he utterly destroyed every person in it, he left none remaining; and he did to the king of Makkedah as he had done to the king of Jericho.

29 Then Joshua passed on from Makke'dah, and all Israel with him, to Libnah, and fought against Libnah; 30and the LORD gave it also and its king into the hand of Israel; and he struck it with the edge of the sword, and every person in it; he left none remaining in it; and he did to its king as he had done to the king of Jericho.

31 And Joshua passed on from Libnah, and all Israel with him, to La'chish, and laid siege to it, and assaulted it: 32and the LORD gave La'chish into the hand of Israel, and he took it on the second day, and struck it with the edge of the sword, and every person in it, as he had done to Libnah.

33 Then Horam king of Gezer came up to help La'chish; and Joshua struck him and his people, until he left none remaining.

34 And Joshua passed on with all Israel from La'chish to Eg'lon; and they laid siege to it, and assaulted it; 35and they took it on that day, and struck it with the edge of the sword; and every person in it he utterly destroyed that day, as he had done to La'chish.

36 Then Joshua went up with all Israel from Eg'lon to He'bron; and they assaulted it, 37and took it, and struck it with the edge of the sword, and its king and its towns, and every person in it; he left none remaining, as he had done to Eg'lon, and utterly destroyed it with every person in it.

38 Then Joshua, with all Israel, turned back to De'bir and assaulted it, 39and he took it with its king and all its towns; and they struck them with the edge of the sword, and utterly destroyed every person in it; he left none remaining; as he had done to Heb'ron and to Libnah and its king, so he did to De'bir and to its king.

40 So Joshua defeated the whole land, the hill country and the Neg'eb and the lowland and the slopes, and all their kings; he left none remaining, but utterly destroyed all that breathed, as the LORD God of Israel commanded. 41And Joshua defeated them from Ka'desh-bar'nea to Gaza, and all the country of Go'shen, as far as Gib'eon. 42And Joshua took all these kings and their land at one time, because the LORD God of Israel fought for Israel. 43Then Joshua returned, and all Israel with him, to the camp at Gilgal.

The United Kings of Northern Canaan Defeated

11 When Jabin king of Ha'zor heard of this, he sent to Jo'bab king of Madon, and to the king of Shimron, and to the king of Ach'shaph, 2and to the kings who were in the northern hill country, and in the Ar'abah south of Chin'neroth, and in the lowland, and in Na'photh-dor on the west, 3to

---

10:26 hung them: I.e., displayed their executed corpses. See note on 8:29. **until evening:** The bodies have to be buried by sunset, lest the land become defiled (Deut 21:22–23).

10:27 great stones: Another rock monument to remind later generations of the Conquest (4:9, 20; 7:26; 8:29).

10:28–39 Joshua leads Israel through southern Canaan, sacking six more cities and leaving no survivors in his wake. Once again, his tribal army proves invincible, for the Lord is fighting on its side (10:42).

10:40–42 A summary of Israel's victories thus far achieved. Comparative studies of Near Eastern war annals have shown that these types of synopsis statements are typically overstated for rhetorical effect. Taken literally, it sounds as though Israel has captured the full extent of Canaan, and all opposition has been eliminated. However, ancient readers of Joshua, being familiar with this literary convention, would have recognized that the author was using hyperbole rather than manipulating history. This is confirmed by later passages in the book, in which the author openly acknowledges the incompleteness of the Conquest (13:1–7; 15:63; 16:10; 17:11–18). • Catholic teaching holds that interpretation of Scripture must consider the "mode of speech" employed by the inspired authors in order to ascertain the meaning of the biblical writings, since truth is conveyed in different ways by different literary genres and techniques (Vatican II, *Dei Verbum* 12).

10:40 Negeb: The wilderness that stretches over the deep south of Canaan. **destroyed all that breathed:** In accord with the military policy outlined in Deut 20:16–18. See essay: *The Conquest of Canaan* at Josh 6.

10:41 Goshen: In southern Canaan (11:16). The reference is not to the fertile Egyptian Delta, where the Israelites lived before the Exodus (Gen 47:27).

10:43 Gilgal: See note on 4:19.

11:1–15 The northern campaign. Joshua's forces obliterate an alliance of northern cities that have banded together to crush the incoming Israelites. It is an impressive coalition of troops assembled from upper and lower Galilee, and the odds weigh heavily against an Israelite victory; nevertheless, Joshua wins the day with the supernatural help of Yahweh.

11:1 Jabin: A dynastic name, borne also by a later king of Hazor in the time of the Judges (Judg 4:2). **Hazor:** A major city in northern Galilee deemed the "head" of several Canaanite kingdoms in the region (11:10). It is with some certainty located at modern Tell el-Qedah. Although Hazor was large and well-fortified, sprawling over 200 acres, archaeology has shown that it was destroyed multiple times in the Middle and Late Bronze Ages, between ca. 1650 and 1200 B.C.

the Canaanites in the east and the west, the Am′-orites, the Hittites, the Per′izzites, and the Jeb′usites in the hill country, and the Hi′vites under Hermon in the land of Mizpah. ⁴And they came out, with all their troops, a great host, in number like the sand that is upon the seashore, with very many horses and chariots. ⁵And all these kings joined their forces, and came and encamped together at the waters of Me′rom, to fight with Israel.

6 And the LORD said to Joshua, "Do not be afraid of them, for tomorrow at this time I will give over all of them, slain, to Israel; you shall hamstring their horses, and burn their chariots with fire." ⁷So Joshua came suddenly upon them with all his people of war, by the waters of Me′rom, and fell upon them. ⁸And the LORD gave them into the hand of Israel, who struck them and chased them as far as Great Sidon and Mis′rephoth-ma′im, and eastward as far as the valley of Mizpeh; and they struck them, until they left none remaining. ⁹And Joshua did to them as the LORD bade him; he hamstrung their horses, and burned their chariots with fire.

10 And Joshua turned back at that time, and took Ha′zor, and struck its king with the sword; for Hazor formerly was the head of all those kingdoms. ¹¹And they put to the sword all who were in it, utterly destroying them; there was none left that breathed, and he burned Ha′zor with fire. ¹²And all the cities of those kings, and all their kings, Joshua took, and struck them with the edge of the sword, utterly destroying them, as Moses the servant of the LORD had commanded. ¹³But none of the cities that stood

---

11:4 chariots: Each one carried two people, a driver and an armed warrior, who worked together as a team. This type of advanced military technology was not found in Israel until the time of the monarchy (2 Sam 8:4; 15:1; 1 Kings 9:19). It is nothing short of miraculous that the foot soldiers of Israel are able to vanquish a horse-and-chariot army.

11:5 waters of Merom: A stream that flows beside the battlefield into the northwest side of the Sea of Galilee (Chinnereth).

11:8 Sidon and Misrephoth-maim: Both are northwest of Galilee on the Mediterranean coast, the former north of

the latter. **valley of Mizpeh:** Directly north of Galilee near the source of the Jordan River.

11:11 utterly destroying: Israel is again engaged in *ḥerem* warfare (Deut 20:16–18). See word study: *Devoted* at 6:17.

11:13 Hazor only: Joshua leaves most of the Canaanite cities intact so that the Israelites can occupy them (24:13; Deut 19:1–2). The fiery destruction of Hazor is an exception to this general policy, as is the overthrow of Jericho (6:24) and Ai (8:28).

CONQUEST OF NORTHERN CANAAN (JOSHUA 11)

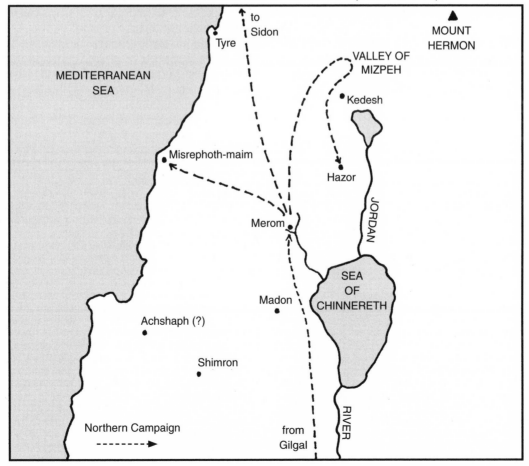

on mounds did Israel burn, except Ha′zor only; that Joshua burned. ¹⁴And all the spoil of these cities and the cattle, the sons of Israel took for their booty; but every man they struck with the edge of the sword, until they had destroyed them, and they did not leave any that breathed. ¹⁵As the LORD had commanded Moses his servant, so Moses commanded Joshua, and so Joshua did; he left nothing undone of all that the LORD had commanded Moses.

Summary of Joshua's Conquests

16 So Joshua took all that land, the hill country and all the Neg′eb and all the land of Go′shen and the lowland and the Ar′abah and the hill country of Israel and its lowland ¹⁷from Mount Ha′lak, that rises toward Se′ir, as far as Ba′al-gad in the valley of Lebanon below Mount Hermon. And he took all their kings, and struck them, and put them to death. ¹⁸Joshua made war a long time with all those kings. ¹⁹There was not a city that made peace with the sons of Israel, except the Hi′vites, the inhabitants of Gib′eon; they took all in battle. ²⁰For it was the LORD's doing to harden their hearts that they should come against Israel in battle, in order that they should be utterly destroyed, and should receive no mercy but be exterminated, as the LORD commanded Moses.

21 And Joshua came at that time, and wiped out the An′akim from the hill country, from He′bron, from De′bir, from A′nab, and from all the hill country of Judah, and from all the hill country of Israel; Joshua utterly destroyed them with their cities. ²²There was none of the An′akim left in the land of the sons of Israel; only in Gaza, in Gath, and in Ashdod, did some remain. ²³So Joshua took the whole land, according to all that the LORD had spoken to Moses; and Joshua gave it for an inheritance to Israel according to their tribal allotments. And the land had rest from war.

The Kings Conquered by Moses

12 Now these are the kings of the land, whom the sons of Israel defeated, and took possession of their land beyond the Jordan toward the sunrising, from the valley of the Arnon to Mount Hermon, with all the Ar′abah eastward: ²Si′hon king of the Am′orites who dwelt at Heshbon, and ruled from Aro′er, which is on the edge of the valley of the Arnon, and from the middle of the valley as far as the river Jabbok, the boundary of the Am′monites, that is, half of Gilead, ³and the Ar′abah to the Sea of Chin′neroth eastward, and in the direction of Beth-jesh′imoth, to the sea of the Arabah, the Salt Sea, southward to the foot of the slopes of Pisgah; ⁴and Og* king of Bashan, one of the remnant of the Reph′aim, who dwelt at Ash′taroth and at Ed′re-i ⁵and ruled over Mount Hermon and Sal′ecah and all Bashan to the boundary of the Gesh′urites and the Ma-ac′athites, and over half of Gilead to the boundary of Si′hon king of Heshbon. ⁶Moses, the servant of the LORD, and the sons of Israel defeated them; and Moses the servant of the LORD gave their land for a possession to the Reubenites and the Gadites and the half-tribe of Manas′seh.

The Kings Conquered by Joshua

7 And these are the kings of the land whom Joshua and the sons of Israel defeated on the west side of the Jordan, from Ba′al-gad in the valley of Lebanon to Mount Ha′lak, that rises toward Se′ir (and Joshua gave their land to the tribes of Israel as a possession according to their allotments, ⁸in the hill country, in the lowland, in the Ar′abah, in the slopes, in the wilderness, and in the Neg′eb, the land of the Hittites, the Am′orites, the Canaanites, the Per′izzites, the Hi′vites, and the Jeb′usites): ⁹the king of Jericho, one; the king of Ai, which is beside Bethel, one; ¹⁰the king of Jerusalem, one; the king of He′bron, one; ¹¹the king of

---

11:14 spoil: Allowance is made for the collection of plunder, as at the battle of Ai (8:2).

11:17 Halak ... Hermon: Mountain peaks that mark the southern and northern extent of the land claimed by Joshua. Halak rises in the southern wilderness near Kadesh-barnea, and Hermon rises northeast of Canaan with its western foothills sloping down toward the headwaters of the Jordan.

11:18 a long time: Approximately seven years. See note on 14:10.

11:20 harden their hearts: The sovereignty of God works even in the lives of Israel's enemies. In a way beyond our comprehension, the Lord can accomplish his plan through the actions of persons bent on evil without either overriding their free will or diminishing their moral responsibility. This mystery was earlier displayed through the hardened heart of Pharaoh in the plague narratives of Exodus. See note on Ex 4:21.

11:21 the Anakim: Descendants of Anak, known in biblical antiquity as fearsome warriors of magnificent size and strength. Years earlier, sightings of the Anakim in Canaan caused the Exodus generation (minus Joshua and Caleb) to

reel back in fear and refuse to fight for the Promised Land (Num 13:28, 32–33; Deut 1:28; 2:10).

11:23 the land had rest: The relative cessation of conflict sets the stage for dividing up the land for settlement (chaps. 13–19). See note on 1:13.

12:1–24 An inventory of defeated Canaanite kings. Moses dethroned two kings east of the Jordan (12:1–6), and Joshua ousted 31 kings west of the Jordan (12:7–24). Several cities and rulers in this list are not elsewhere mentioned in the book—an indication that the war stories of chaps. 6–11 constitute a selective overview of the Israelite campaigns. For the significance of placing the triumphs of Moses and Joshua side by side, see note on 1:5.

12:1 the Arnon: A river canyon that runs into the eastern side of the Dead Sea and marks the southern limit of Israel's territory in the Transjordan. **Mount Hermon:** Rises northeast of the Sea of Galilee and marks the northern limit of Israelite territory at this time.

12:6 Reubenites ... Manasseh: Allotted lands east of the Jordan in Num 32:1–42.

12:7 the west side: The land of Canaan proper (Num 33:51). Scholars sometimes call it the Cisjordan. For the northern and southern extent of this territory, see note on 11:17.

---

*Gk: Heb *the boundary of Og.*

Jarmuth, one; the king of La′chish, one; ¹²the king of Eg′lon, one; the king of Gezer, one; ¹³the king of De′bir, one; the king of Geder, one; ¹⁴the king of Hormah, one; the king of Ar′ad, one; ¹⁵the king of Libnah, one; the king of Adul′lam, one; ¹⁶the king of Makke′dah, one; the king of Bethel, one; ¹⁷the king of Tap′pu-ah, one; the king of He′pher, one; ¹⁸the king of A′phek, one; the king of Lashar′on, one; ¹⁹the king of Madon, one; the king of Ha′zor, one; ²⁰the king of Shim′ron-me′ron, one; the king of Ach′shaph, one; ²¹the king of Ta′anach, one; the king of Megid′do, one; ²²the king of Ke′desh, one; the king of Jok′ne-am in Carmel, one; ²³the king of Dor in Na′phath-dor, one; the king of Goi′im in Galilee,ᶠ one; ²⁴the king of Tirzah, one: in all, thirty-one kings.

Still Unconquered Parts of Canaan

13 *Now Joshua was old and advanced in years; and the LORD said to him, "You are old and advanced in years, and there remains yet very much land to be possessed. ²This is the land that yet remains: all the regions of the Philis′tines, and all those of the Gesh′urites ³(from the Shi′hor, which is east of Egypt, northward to the boundary of Ek′ron, it is reckoned as Canaanite; there are five

rulers of the Philis′tines, those of Gaza, Ash′dod, Ash′kelon, Gath, and Ek′ron), and those of the Avvim, ⁴in the south, all the land of the Canaanites, and Me-ar′ah which belongs to the Sido′nians, to A′phek, to the boundary of the Am′orites, ⁵and the land of the Geb′alites, and all Lebanon, toward the sunrising, from Ba′al-gad below Mount Hermon to the entrance of Ha′math, ⁶all the inhabitants of the hill country from Lebanon to Mis′rephoth-ma′im, even all the Sido′nians. I will myself drive them out from before the sons of Israel; only allot the land to Israel for an inheritance, as I have commanded you. ⁷Now therefore divide this land for an inheritance to the nine tribes and half the tribe of Manas′seh."

8 With the other half of the tribe of Manas′sehᵍ the Reubenites and the Gadites received their inheritance, which Moses gave them, beyond the Jordan eastward, as Moses the servant of the LORD gave them: ⁹from Aro′er, which is on the edge of the valley of the Arnon, and the city that is in the middle of the valley, and all the tableland of Med′eba as far as Di′bon; ¹⁰and all the cities of Si′hon king of the Am′orites, who reigned in Heshbon, as far as the boundary of the Am′monites; ¹¹and Gilead, and the region of the Gesh′urites and Ma-ac′athites, and all

---

13:1–21:45 Nine chapters outline the division of Canaan among the Israelite tribes. Towns and territorial boundaries are assigned to each, although some of these locations are no longer known with certainty today. Still, the general picture is clear: two and a half tribes settle east of the Jordan (13:8–31), nine and a half tribes acquire lands west of the Jordan (14:1–19:48), and the tribe of Levi disperses to 48 cities located throughout the tribal allotments (21:1–42). Only a list of towns is supplied for the tribes of Simeon and Issachar. Apportionment of the land by lot follows the Lord's directive in Num 26:52–56. • Allegorically, as Joshua leads the people into the land and gives them a temporary inheritance, so Jesus, after his holy Resurrection, brings us into the good land to give us an everlasting inheritance (St. Justin Martyr, *Dialogue with Trypho* 113).

13:1 Joshua was old: His contemporary, Caleb, was 85 years old (14:10). **very much land:** Indicates that the war to seize possession of Canaan is not finished. Unconquered lands consist mainly of Philistia on the southwest coast (13:2–3) as well as Phoenicia and lower Syria to the north of Galilee (13:4–5). These regions would not be fully subdued until the days of David and Solomon (Geshurites, 1 Sam 27:8; Philistines, 2 Sam 8:1; Syrians, 2 Sam 8:6; 1 Kings 4:21). See note on 1:4.

13:2 Philistines: Migratory peoples from the Mediterranean who settled on the coastlands of Canaan in the second millennium B.C. See note on Judg 3:3.

13:5 entrance of Hamath: North of Damascus in lower Syria.

13:8–13 Before the invasion of Canaan, Moses allotted Reuben, Gad, and half of Manasseh homelands east of the Jordan (Num 32:1–42). The Transjordan is thus partitioned

into three tribal territories, with Reuben in the south (13:15–23), Gad in the central region (13:24–28), and half-Manasseh assigned to the north (13:29–31). Israel seized these lands from the Amorite kings, Sihon and Og (Num 21:21–35).

WORD STUDY

Inheritance (13:7)

nahalah (Heb.): means "possession", "inheritance", or "heritage" and refers to property that is passed down from generation to generation within a family (Gen 31:14; 1 Kings 21:3). Scripture extends this basic idea in several different ways. (1) The Promised Land of Canaan is the inheritance that Father Yahweh wills to the children of Israel by covenant (Deut 4:21). A heritage of land is thus assigned to each individual tribe (Josh 11:23) that, by law, must be passed down within that tribe (Num 36:7). (2) The tribe of Levi is a special case, since it receives no land like the other tribes. Instead, its members inherit the priesthood (18:7) as well as portions of the animal and food offerings that the Israelites bring to the sanctuary (Num 18:21–24; Josh 13:14). (3) Ultimately, the Lord himself is the inheritance of his people. Not only do priests and Levites have God as their possession by virtue of their ministerial office (Num 18:20; Josh 13:14), but the Psalter teaches that Yahweh is the heritage of all the righteous (Ps 16:5). This paves the way for the gospel, which promises the faithful an eternal inheritance kept safe in heaven (Heb 9:15; 1 Pet 1:4).

ᶠ Gk: Heb *Gilgal.*
ᵍ Cn: Heb *With it.*
*13–21: This section consists of topographical indications: the possessions and boundaries of the tribes and other ethnic groups, and a list of the cities of refuge.

Mount Hermon, and all Bashan to Sal'ecah; ¹²all the kingdom of Og in Bashan, who reigned in Ash'taroth and in Ed're-i (he alone was left of the remnant of the Reph'aim); these Moses had defeated and driven out. ¹³Yet the sons of Israel did not drive out the Gesh'urites or the Ma-ac'athites; but Ge'shur and Ma'acath dwell in the midst of Israel to this day.

14 To the tribe of Levi alone Moses gave no inheritance; the offerings by fire to the LORD God of Israel are their inheritance, as he said to him.

The Territory of Reuben

15 And Moses gave an inheritance to the tribe of the Reubenites according to their families. ¹⁶So their territory was from Aro'er, which is on the edge of the valley of the Arnon, and the city that is in the middle of the valley, and all the tableland by Med'eba; ¹⁷with Heshbon, and all its cities that are in the tableland; Di'bon, and Ba'moth-ba'al, and Beth-ba'al-me'on, ¹⁸and Ja'haz, and Ked'emoth, and Meph'a-ath, ¹⁹and Kir″iatha'im, and Sibmah, and Ze'reth-sha'har on the hill of the valley, ²⁰and Beth-pe'or, and the slopes of Pisgah, and Beth-jesh'imoth, ²¹that is, all the cities of the tableland, and all the kingdom of Si'hon king of the Am'orites, who reigned in Heshbon, whom Moses defeated with the leaders of Mid'ian, E'vi and Re'kem and Zur and Hur and Reba, the princes of Si'hon, who dwelt in the land. ²²Balaam also, the son of Beor, the soothsayer, the sons of Israel killed with the sword among the rest of their slain. ²³And the border of the people of Reuben was the Jordan as a boundary. This was the inheritance of the Reubenites, according to their families with their cities and villages.

The Territory of Gad

24 And Moses gave an inheritance also to the tribe of the Gadites, according to their families. ²⁵Their territory was Ja'zer, and all the cities of Gilead, and half the land of the Am'monites, to Aro'er, which is east of Rabbah, ²⁶and from Heshbon to Ra'math-miz'peh and Bet'onim, and from Ma″hana'im to the territory of De'bir,ʰ ²⁷and in the valley Beth-

ha'ram, Beth-nim'rah, Succoth, and Za'phon, the rest of the kingdom of Si'hon king of Heshbon, having the Jordan as a boundary, to the lower end of the Sea of Chin'nereth, eastward beyond the Jordan. ²⁸This is the inheritance of the Gadites according to their families, with their cities and villages.

The Territory of the Half-tribe of Manasseh (East)

29 And Moses gave an inheritance to the half-tribe of Manas'-seh; it was allotted to the half-tribe of the Manas'sites according to their families. ³⁰Their region extended from Ma″hana'im, through all Bashan, the whole kingdom of Og king of Bashan, and all the towns of Ja'ir, which are in Bashan, sixty cities, ³¹and half Gilead, and Ash'taroth, and Ed're-i, the cities of the kingdom of Og in Bashan; these were allotted to the people of Ma'chir the son of Manas'seh for the half of the Ma'chirites according to their families.

32 These are the inheritances which Moses distributed in the plains of Moab, beyond the Jordan east of Jericho. ³³But to the tribe of Levi Moses gave no inheritance; the LORD God of Israel is their inheritance, as he said to them.

The Distribution of Territory West of the Jordan

14 And these are the inheritances which the sons of Israel received in the land of Canaan, which Elea'zar the priest, and Joshua the son of Nun, and the heads of the fathers' houses of the tribes of the sons of Israel distributed to them. ²Their inheritance was by lot, as the LORD had commanded Moses for the nine and one-half tribes. ³For Moses had given an inheritance to the two and one-half tribes beyond the Jordan; but to the Levites he gave no inheritance among them. ⁴For the people of Joseph were two tribes, Manas'seh and E'phraim; and no portion was given to the Levites in the land, but only cities to dwell in, with their pasture lands for their cattle and their substance. ⁵The sons of Israel did as the LORD commanded Moses; they allotted the land.

13:13 did not drive out: Implies that Israel stops short of full obedience to the Lord's will. This and similar notations later in the book set the stage for troubles down the road from the Canaanite peoples left in the land (15:63; 16:10; 17:12–13; 23:12–13).

13:14 no inheritance: The ministerial tribe of Levi is the one landless tribe in Israel. Instead of territory, it receives 48 cities dispersed throughout the length and breadth of Canaan (Num 35:1–8). See word study: *Inheritance* at 13:7.

13:15 Reubenites: Descendants of Jacob's oldest son, Reuben (Gen 35:22–23).

13:21–22 Moses warred against the five kings of **Midian** and cut down the soothsayer **Balaam** in Num 31:1–12.

13:24 Gadites: Descendants of Jacob's seventh son, Gad (Gen 30:10–11).

13:27 Sea of Chinnereth: Ancient name for the Sea of Galilee in northeast Canaan.

13:29 half-tribe of Manasseh: Descendants of Jacob's grandson Manasseh, who was born to Joseph in Egypt (Gen 46:20; 48:5).

14:1 Eleazar: Son and successor of Aaron, the first high priest, who died before the start of the Conquest (Num 20:22–29). Eleazar's role in parceling out the land is connected with the sacred lots, called Urim and Thummim, which were kept in the linen breastpiece of the high priest (Ex 28:30). Joshua will consult him on important matters that require these lots to discern the Lord's will (Num 27:21).

14:4 two tribes: Descended from the two sons born to Joseph in Egypt, Manasseh and Ephraim (Gen 46:20). Their adoption into the family of Israel kept the number of lay tribes at 12 after the tribe of Levi was set apart for liturgical ministry (Num 3:6–13). See note on Gen 48:1–22. **cities:** Specified by name in 21:8–42.

ʰ Gk Syr Vg: Heb *Lidebir.*

Hebron Allotted to Caleb

6 Then the people of Judah came to Joshua at Gilgal; and Caleb the son of Jephun'neh the Ken'izzite said to him, "You know what the LORD said to Moses the man of God in Ka'desh-bar'nea concerning you and me. 7I was forty years old when Moses the servant of the LORD sent me from Ka'desh-bar'nea to spy out the land; and I brought him word again as it was in my heart. 8But my brethren who went up with me made the heart of the people melt; yet I wholly followed the LORD my God. 9And Moses swore on that day, saying, 'Surely the land on which your foot has trodden shall be an inheritance for you and your children for ever, because you have wholly followed the LORD my God.' 10And now, behold, the LORD has kept me alive, as he said, these forty-five years since the time that the LORD spoke this word to Moses, while Israel walked in the wilderness; and now, behold, I am this day eighty-five years old. 11I am still as strong to this day as I was in the day that Moses sent me; my strength now is as my strength was then, for war, and for going and coming. 12So now give me this hill country of which the LORD spoke on that day; for you heard on that day how the An'akim were there, with great fortified cities: it may be that the LORD will be with me, and I shall drive them out as the LORD said."

13 Then Joshua blessed him; and he gave He'bron to Caleb the son of Jephun'neh for an inheritance. 14So He'bron became the inheritance of Caleb the son of Jephun'neh the Ken'izzite to this day, because he wholly followed the LORD, the God of Israel. 15Now the name of He'bron formerly was Kir'iath-ar'ba;[i] this Arba was the greatest man among the An'akim. And the land had rest from war.

The Territory of Judah

15 The lot for the tribe of the people of Judah according to their families reached southward to the boundary of E'dom, to the wilderness of Zin at the farthest south. 2And their south boundary ran from the end of the Salt Sea, from the bay that faces southward; 3it goes out southward of the ascent of Akrab'bim, passes along to Zin, and goes up south of Ka'desh-bar'nea, along by Hezron, up to Addar, turns about to Karka, 4passes along to Azmon, goes out by the Brook of Egypt, and comes to its end at the sea. This shall be your south boundary. 5And the east boundary is the Salt Sea, to the mouth of the Jordan. And the boundary on the north side runs from the bay of the sea at the mouth of the Jordan; 6and the boundary goes up to Beth-hog'lah, and passes along north of Beth-ar'abah; and the boundary goes up to the stone of Bohan the son of Reuben; 7and the boundary goes up to De'bir from the Valley of A'chor, and so northward, turning toward Gilgal, which is opposite the ascent of Adum'mim, which is on the south side of the valley; and the boundary passes along to the waters of En-she'mesh, and ends at En-ro'gel; 8then the boundary goes up by the valley of the son of Hinnom at the southern shoulder of the Jeb'usite (that is, Jerusalem); and the boundary goes up to the top of the mountain that lies over against the valley of Hinnom, on the west, at the northern end of the valley of Reph'aim; 9then the boundary extends from the top of the mountain to the spring of the Waters of Nephto'ah, and from there to the cities of Mount E'phron; then the boundary bends round to Ba'alah (that is, Kir'iath-je'arim); 10and the boundary circles west of Ba'alah to Mount Se'ir, passes along to the northern shoulder of Mount Je'arim (that is, Ches'alon), and goes down to Beth-she'mesh, and passes along by Timnah; 11the boundary goes out to the shoulder of the hill north of Ek'ron, then the boundary bends round to Shik'keron, and passes along to Mount Ba'alah, and

---

14:6–15: Num 13:6, 30; 14:6, 24, 30.

14:6–15 Joshua grants Caleb the city of Hebron as his inheritance. Recall that Joshua and Caleb were the only two adults of the Exodus generation to cross over into Canaan, and this because their faith in Yahweh overpowered their fear of the Canaanites (Num 13–14). The Lord prolonged Caleb's life (14:10) and preserved his strength (14:11) in order to give him the blessing of a place in the Promised Land.

14:6 Gilgal: Israel's base camp since crossing the Jordan (4:19). **the Kenizzite:** Perhaps an indication that Caleb has genealogical ties with the Edomite chieftain, Kenaz (Gen 36:15; Num 32:12). Caleb is likewise closely linked to Judah: he was chosen to represent the tribe of Judah in Num 13:6, and he is listed in the genealogy of Judah in 1 Chron 4:15.

14:10 forty-five years: Since the rebellion of Israel at Kadesh in Num 14. This implies that Joshua's campaign against Canaan lasts about seven years, since Israel invades the land about 38 years after leaving Kadesh (Deut 2:14).

14:12 the Anakim: The descendants of Anak. See note on 11:21.

14:13 Hebron: In the southern highlands of Palestine, over 20 miles south of Jerusalem. The Bible remembers this city as the burial place of the Patriarchs and their wives (Gen 23:19; 49:29–32).

14:15 the land had rest: Repeats the earlier statement in 11:23. It suggests that Caleb's request for an inheritance is made before the war is over rather than afterward. Most likely, the author places the episode here because of its thematic links with the allotment of the land.

15:1–63 The tribe of **Judah** inherits land in southern Canaan between the Dead Sea on the east (the Salt Sea, 15:5) and the Mediterranean Sea on the west (the Great Sea, 15:12). Its northern border skirts the slopes of Jerusalem (15:63), and its southern border forms the bottom edge of the Promised Land (compare 15:2–4 with Num 34:3–5). Judah stands first in line to receive its inheritance, perhaps because it holds the distinction of being the royal and messianic tribe of Israel (Gen 49:8–10; Jn 4:22; Heb 7:14).

15:4 Brook of Egypt: Not the Nile River, but a seasonal stream that flows across the top of the Sinai Peninsula (modern Wadi el-Arish).

---

[i] That is *The city of Arba.*

goes out to Jab'neel; then the boundary comes to an end at the sea. ¹²And the west boundary was the Great Sea with its coast-line. This is the boundary round about the people of Judah according to their families.

Caleb Occupies His Portion

13 According to the commandment of the LORD to Joshua, he gave to Caleb the son of Jephun'neh a portion among the people of Judah, Kir'iath-ar'ba, that is, He'bron (Arba was the father of A'nak). ¹⁴And Caleb drove out from there the three sons of A'nak, She'shai and Ahi'man and Talmai, the descendants of Anak. ¹⁵And he went up from there against the inhabitants of De'bir; now the name of Debir formerly was Kir'iath-se'pher. ¹⁶And Caleb said, "Whoever strikes Kir'iath-se'pher, and takes it, to him will I give Ach'sah my daughter as wife." ¹⁷And Oth'ni-el the son of Ke'naz, the brother of Caleb, took it; and he gave him Ach'sah his daughter as wife. ¹⁸When she came to him, she urged him to ask her father for a field; and she alighted from her donkey, and Caleb said to her, "What do you wish?" ¹⁹She said to him, "Give me a present; since you have set me in the land of the Neg'eb, give me also springs of water." And Caleb gave her the upper springs and the lower springs.

The Towns of Judah

20 This is the inheritance of the tribe of the people of Judah according to their families. ²¹The cities belonging to the tribe of the people of Judah in the extreme South, toward the boundary of E'dom, were Kab'zeel, E'der, Jagur, ²²Kinah, Dimo'nah, Ada'dah, ²³Ke'desh, Ha'zor, Ithnan, ²⁴Ziph, Telem, Be-a'loth, ²⁵Ha'zor-hadat'tah, Ker'i-oth-hez'ron (that is, Ha'zor), ²⁶A'mam, Shema, Mo'ladah, ²⁷Ha'zar-gad'-dah, Heshmon, Beth-pel'et, ²⁸Ha'-zar-shu'al, Be'er-she'ba, Biziothi'ah, ²⁹Ba'alah, I'im, E'zem, ³⁰Elto'lad, Che'sil, Hormah, ³¹Zik'-lag, Madman'nah, Sansan'nah, ³²Leba'oth, Shilhim, A'in, and Rimmon: in all, twenty-nine cities, with their villages.

33 And in the lowland, Esh'ta-ol, Zorah, Ash-nah, ³⁴Zano'ah, En-gan'nim, Tap'pu-ah, E'nam, ³⁵Jarmuth, Adul'lam, Socoh, Aze'kah, ³⁶Sha"ara'im, Aditha'im, Gede'rah, Gede'rotha"im: fourteen cities with their villages.

37 Ze'nan, Hadash'ah, Mig'-dal-gad, ³⁸Di'lean, Mizpeh, Jok'-the-el, ³⁹La'chish, Bozkath, Eg'lon, ⁴⁰Cabbon, Lahmam, Chitlish, ⁴¹Gede'roth, Beth-da'-gon, Na'amah, and Makke'dah: sixteen cities with their villages.

42 Libnah, E'ther, A'shan, ⁴³Iphtah, Ash'nah, Nezib, ⁴⁴Kei'-lah, Ach'zib, and Mare'shah: nine cities with their villages.

45 Ek'ron, with its towns and its villages; ⁴⁶from Ek'ron to the sea, all that were by the side of Ash'dod, with their villages.

47 Ash'dod, its towns and its villages; Gaza, its towns and its villages; to the Brook of Egypt, and the Great Sea with its coast-line.

48 And in the hill country, Sha'mir, Jat'tir, Socoh, ⁴⁹Dannah, Kir'iath-san'nah (that is, De'bir), ⁵⁰A'nab, Esh'temoh, A'nim, ⁵¹Goshen, Holon, and Giloh: eleven cities with their villages.

52 A'rab, Du'mah, E'shan, ⁵³Ja'-nim, Beth-tap'-pu-ah, Aphe'kah, ⁵⁴Humtah, Kir'iath-ar'ba (that is, He'bron), and Zior: nine cities with their villages.

55 Maon, Carmel, Ziph, Juttah, ⁵⁶Jezre'el, Jok'de-am, Zano'-ah, ⁵⁷Kain, Gib'e-ah, and Timnah: ten cities with their villages.

58 Halhul, Beth-zur, Gedor, ⁵⁹Ma'arath, Beth-a'noth, and El'tekon: six cities with their villages.

60 Kir'iath-ba'al (that is, Kir'-iath-je'arim), and Rabbah: two cities with their villages.

61 In the wilderness, Beth-ar'abah, Middin, Seca'-cah, ⁶²Nibshan, the City of Salt, and En-ge'di: six cities with their villages.

63 But the Jeb'usites, the inhabitants of Jerusalem, the people of Judah could not drive out; so the Jebusites dwell with the people of Judah at Jerusalem to this day.

The Territory of Ephraim

16 The allotment of the descendants of Joseph went from the Jordan by Jericho, east of the waters of Jericho, into the wilderness, going up from Jericho into the hill country to Bethel; ²then going from Bethel to Luz, it passes along to At'aroth, the territory of the Ar'chites; ³then it goes down westward to the territory of the Japh'letites, as far as the territory of Lower Beth-ho'ron, then to Gezer, and it ends at the sea.

15:14–19: Judg 1:10–15, 20. **15:63:** Judg 1:21; 2 Sam 5:6.

15:13 Hebron: Allotted to Caleb by request (14:6–15).

15:16–19 The story of Othni-el and Achsah also appears in Judg 1:12–15.

15:20–62 The cities assigned to Judah fall into four geographical regions: the deep south (15:21–32), the lowlands (15:33–47), the hill country (15:48–60), and the wilderness (15:61–62). The exact location of many of these settlements is no longer known.

15:61 the wilderness: The arid country west of the Dead Sea.

15:63 Jerusalem: On the Judah-Benjamin border (18:28). For a long time, neither tribe could overthrow the fortified settlement established there (Judg 1:21). Judah captured it briefly, but eventually it fell back into Canaanite hands (Judg 1:8). It was David who finally ousted the Jebusites and made Jerusalem the capital of Israel (2 Sam 5:6–9). See note on 10:1.

16:1–17:18 Chapters 16 and 17 delineate the inheritance given to the two Joseph tribes, Ephraim (16:5–10) and Manasseh (17:1–13). Together they acquire a large tract of central Canaan between the Jordan River on the east and the Mediterranean coast on the west. Half of the tribe of Manasseh has already acquired lands east of the Jordan (Num 32:39–42). Second only to Judah, these tribes are among the first to receive lands because Jacob honored them with the first-born birthright that was taken away from his oldest son, Reuben (Gen 48:1–20; 1 Chron 5:1–2).

4 The people of Joseph, Manas'seh and E'phraim, received their inheritance.

5 The territory of the E'ph-raimites by their families was as follows: the boundary of their inheritance on the east was At'aroth-ad'dar as far as Upper Beth-ho'ron, ⁶and the boundary goes thence to the sea; on the north is Michme'thath; then on the east the boundary turns round toward Ta'anath-shi'loh, and passes along beyond it on the east to Jano'ah, ⁷then it goes down from Jano'ah to At'aroth and to Na'arah, and touches Jericho, ending at the Jordan. ⁸From Tap'pu-ah the boundary goes westward to the brook Kanah, and ends at the sea. Such is the inheritance of the tribe of the E'phraimites by their families, ⁹together with the towns which were set apart for the E'phraimites within the inheritance of the Manas'sites, all those towns with their villages. ¹⁰However they did not

---

16:10: Judg 1:29.

16:5–10 The tribe of **Ephraim** inherits the lower part of central Canaan. Joshua himself is an Ephraimite (Num 13:8, 16) and is later buried in Ephraimite territory (24:30).

16:10 did not drive out: Confirms that the Conquest is incomplete (13:1–7). See note on 13:13. **forced labor:** Israel subjugates the surviving Canaanites who did not fall in battle (17:13; Judg 1:28, 33; 1 Kings 9:20–21). • Presumably this is a realization of the curse that Noah pronounced upon Canaan for the wickedness of Ham ("Cursed be Canaan: a slave of slaves shall he be to his brothers", Gen 9:25). Genesis states that Canaan and Israel descended from the brothers Ham (Gen 10:16–20) and Shem, respectively (Abraham, Gen 11:10–26).

DIVISION OF THE PROMISED LAND (JOSHUA 13–19)

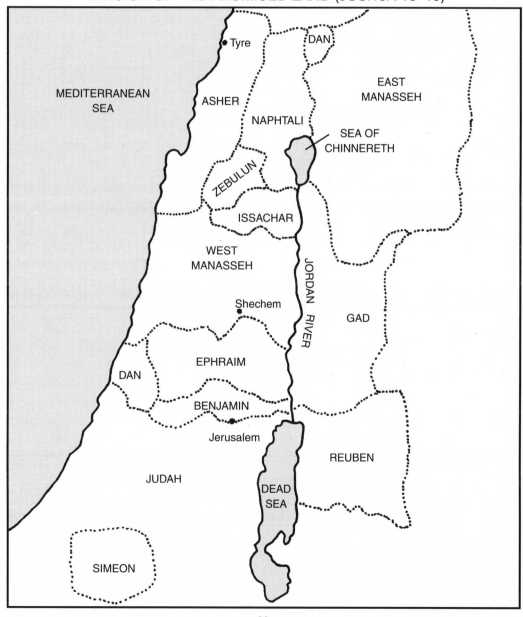

drive out the Canaanites that dwelt in Gezer: so the Canaanites have dwelt in the midst of E′phraim to this day but have become slaves to do forced labor.

The Territory of the Half-tribe
of Manasseh (West)

17 Then allotment was made to the tribe of Manas′seh, for he was the first-born of Joseph. To Ma′chir the first-born of Manasseh, the father of Gilead, were allotted Gilead and Bashan, because he was a man of war. ²And allotments were made to the rest of the tribe of Manas′seh, by their families, Abi-e′zer, He′lek, As′ri-el, She′chem, He′pher, and Shemi′da; these were the male descendants of Manasseh the son of Joseph, by their families.

3 Now Zeloph′ehad the son of He′pher, son of Gilead, son of Ma′chir, son of Manas′seh, had no sons, but only daughters; and these are the names of his daughters: Mahlah, Noah, Hoglah, Milcah, and Tirzah. ⁴They came before Elea′zar the priest and Joshua the son of Nun and the leaders, and said, "The LORD commanded Moses to give us an inheritance along with our brethren." So according to the commandment of the LORD he gave them an inheritance among the brethren of their father. ⁵Thus there fell to Manas′seh ten portions, besides the land of Gilead and Bashan, which is on the other side of the Jordan; ⁶because the daughters of Manas′seh received an inheritance along with his sons. The land of Gilead was allotted to the rest of the Manas′sites.

7 The territory of Manas′seh reached from Asher to Michme′thath, which is east of She′chem; then the boundary goes along southward to the inhabitants of En-tap′pu-ah. ⁸The land of Tap′pu-ah belonged to Manas′seh, but the town of Tappu-ah on the boundary of Manasseh belonged to the sons of E′phraim. ⁹Then the boundary went down to the brook Kanah. The cities here, to the south of the brook, among the cities of Manas′seh, belong to E′phraim. Then the boundary of Manasseh goes on the north side of the brook and ends at the sea;

¹⁰the land to the south being E′phraim's and that to the north being Manas′seh's, with the sea forming its boundary; on the north Asher is reached, and on the east Is′sachar. ¹¹Also in Is′sachar and in Asher Manas′seh had Beth-she′an and its villages, and Ib′leam and its villages, and the inhabitants of Dor and its villages, and the inhabitants of En-dor and its villages, and the inhabitants of Ta′anach and its villages, and the inhabitants of Megid′do and its villages; the third is Na′phath.ʲ ¹²Yet the sons of Manas′seh could not take possession of those cities; but the Canaanites persisted in dwelling in that land. ¹³But when the sons of Israel grew strong, they put the Canaanites to forced labor, and did not utterly drive them out.

The Tribe of Joseph Protests

14 And the tribe of Joseph spoke to Joshua, saying, "Why have you given me but one lot and one portion as an inheritance, although I am a numerous people, since hitherto the LORD has blessed me?" ¹⁵And Joshua said to them, "If you are a numerous people, go up to the forest, and there clear ground for yourselves in the land of the Per′izzites and the Reph′aim, since the hill country of E′phraim is too narrow for you." ¹⁶The tribe of Joseph said, "The hill country is not enough for us; yet all the Canaanites who dwell in the plain have chariots of iron, both those in Beth-she′an and its villages and those in the Valley of Jezre′el." ¹⁷Then Joshua said to the house of Joseph, to E′phraim and Manas′seh, "You are a numerous people, and have great power; you shall not have one lot only, ¹⁸but the hill country shall be yours, for though it is a forest, you shall clear it and possess it to its farthest borders; for you shall drive out the Canaanites, though they have chariots of iron, and though they are strong."

The Territories of the Remaining Tribes

18 Then the whole congregation of the sons of Israel assembled at Shiloh, and set up the tent of meeting there; the land lay subdued before them.

17:3, 4: Num 26:33; 27:1–7. 17:11–13: Judg 1:27–28.

17:1–13 Half of the tribe of **Manasseh** receives its inheritance west of the Jordan. Their territory in north-central Canaan is the second largest tribal allotment after that given to Judah (15:1–12).

17:1 the first-born: Manasseh was the older of Joseph's two sons (Gen 41:50–52). **Gilead and Bashan:** Lands east of the Jordan where the other half of the Manasseh tribe settles (13:29–31).

17:4 give us an inheritance: Moses ruled that daughters could inherit the lands of their father if he should die without a male heir (Num 27:1–11). The promise to allot land to the daughters of Zelophehad, who acquire lands in the north, parallels his promise to allot land to Caleb, who receives his inheritance in the south (14:6–15).

17:5 ten portions: Allotted to the six clans of Manasseh (17:2), one of which is divided five ways among the five daughters of Zelophehad (17:3).

17:11 Beth-shean … Naphath: Manasseh fails to gain control over several of these towns during the settlement period (17:12; Judg 1:27).

17:13 forced labor: On the subjugation of Canaanites, see note on 16:10.

17:18 clear it: Deforesting parts of the hill country will create more living and farming space for the populous Joseph tribes. **drive out:** Ephraim and Manasseh will overcome the superior might of the Canaanites with Yahweh fighting on their side (21:43–44).

18:1–10 Joshua dispatches a team of surveyors to map out seven territories for the seven tribes still waiting to receive land—Benjamin, Simeon, Zebulun, Issachar, Asher, Naphtali, and Dan. Information about the towns and topography of these regions is recorded in a written document (18:9).

18:1 Shiloh: In the territory of Ephraim about 20 miles north of Jerusalem. It is with some certainty located at modern Khirbet Seilun. For reasons unstated, Shiloh is chosen to be the host city for the Mosaic Tabernacle, and as such it becomes the primary place of worship and tribal assembly for much of the long

---

ʲ Heb obscure.

2 There remained among the sons of Israel seven tribes whose inheritance had not yet been apportioned. ³So Joshua said to the sons of Israel, "How long will you be slack to go in and take possession of the land, which the LORD, the God of your fathers, has given you? ⁴Provide three men from each tribe, and I will send them out that they may set out and go up and down the land, writing a description of it with a view to their inheritances, and then come to me. ⁵They shall divide it into seven portions, Judah continuing in his territory on the south, and the house of Joseph in their territory on the north. ⁶And you shall describe the land in seven divisions and bring the description here to me; and I will cast lots for you here before the LORD our God. ⁷The Levites have no portion among you, for the priesthood of the LORD is their heritage; and Gad and Reuben and half the tribe of Manas'seh have received their inheritance beyond the Jordan eastward, which Moses the servant of the LORD gave them."

8 So the men started on their way; and Joshua charged those who went to write the description of the land, saying, "Go up and down and write a description of the land, and come again to me; and I will cast lots for you here before the LORD in Shiloh." ⁹So the men went and passed up and down in the land and set down in a book a description of it by towns in seven divisions; then they came to Joshua in the camp at Shiloh, ¹⁰and Joshua cast lots for them in Shiloh before the LORD; and there Joshua apportioned the land to the sons of Israel, to each his portion.

The Territory of Benjamin

11 The lot of the tribe of Benjamin according to its families came up, and the territory allotted to it fell between the tribe of Judah and the tribe of Joseph. ¹²On the north side their boundary began at the Jordan; then the boundary goes up to the shoulder north of Jericho, then up through the hill country westward; and it ends at the wilderness of Beth-a'ven. ¹³From there the boundary passes along southward in the direction of Luz, to the shoulder of Luz (the same is Bethel), then the boundary goes down to At'aroth-ad'dar, upon the mountain that lies south of Lower Beth-ho'ron. ¹⁴Then the boundary goes in another direction, turning on the western side southward from the mountain that lies to the south, opposite Beth-ho'ron, and it ends at Kir'iath-ba'al (that is, Kir'iath-je'arim), a city belonging to the tribe of Judah. This forms the western side. ¹⁵And the southern side begins at the outskirts of Kir'iath-je'arim; and the boundary goes from there to E'phron,ᵏ to the spring of the Waters of Nephto'ah; ¹⁶then the boundary goes down to the border of the mountain that overlooks the valley of the son of Hinnom, which is at the north end of the valley of Reph'aim; and it then goes down the valley of Hinnom, south of the shoulder of the Jeb'usites, and downward to En-ro'gel; ¹⁷then it bends in a northerly direction going on to En-she'mesh, and thence goes to Geli'loth, which is opposite the ascent of Adum'mim; then it goes down to the stone of Bohan the son of Reuben; ¹⁸and passing on to the north of the shoulder of Beth-ar'abahˡ it goes down to the Ar'abah; ¹⁹then the boundary passes on to the north of the shoulder of Beth-hog'lah; and the boundary ends at the northern bay of the Salt Sea, at the south end of the Jordan: this is the southern border. ²⁰The Jordan forms its boundary on the eastern side. This is the inheritance of the tribe of Benjamin, according to its families, boundary by boundary round about.

21 Now the cities of the tribe of Benjamin according to their families were Jericho, Beth-hog'-lah, E'mek-ke'ziz, ²²Beth-ar'abah, Zemara'im, Bethel, ²³Avvim, Par'ah, Oph'rah, ²⁴Che'pharam'-moni, Ophni, Ge'ba—twelve cities with their villages: ²⁵Gib'eon, Ra'mah, Be-er'oth, ²⁶Mizpeh, Che-phi'rah, Mozah, ²⁷Re'kem, Ir'peel, Tar'alah, ²⁸Ze'la, Ha-e'leph, Je'busᵐ (that is, Jerusalem), Gib'e-ahⁿ and Kir'iath-je'arimᵒ—fourteen cities with their villages. This is the inheritance of the tribe of Benjamin according to its families.

The Territory of Simeon

19 The second lot came out for Simeon, for the tribe of Simeon, according to its families; and its inheritance was in the midst of the inheritance of the tribe of Judah. ²And it had for its inheritance Be'er-she'ba, Sheba, Mo'ladah, ³Ha'zar-shu'al, Balah, E'zem, ⁴Elto'lad, Be'thul, Hormah, ⁵Zik'-lag, Beth-mar'caboth, Ha'zar-su'sah, ⁶Beth-leba'oth,

---

settlement period (19:51; 22:12; Judg 18:31). Apart from one possible relocation to Shechem in 24:1, the sanctuary seems to have remained at Shiloh into the days of Samuel (1 Sam 1:3).
18:6 I will cast lots: In cooperation with the high priest, Eleazar (19:51). See note on 14:1.
18:7 Levites: The ministerial tribe of Levi is the one tribe not assigned territory in Canaan. See word study: *Inheritance* at 13:7.

ᵏCn See 15:9. Heb *westward.*
ˡGk: Heb *to the shoulder over against the Arabah.*
ᵐGk Syr Vg: Heb *the Jebusite.*
ⁿHeb *Gibeath.*
ᵒGk: Heb *Kiriath.*

18:11-28 The tribe of **Benjamin** inherits a narrow strip of land that is wedged between Judah to the south and the Joseph tribes to the north. Horizontally it stretches from Kiriath-jearim in the west (18:14) to the Jordan River in the east (18:20). Benjaminite territory encompasses 26 cities, one of which is Jerusalem (18:21-28).
19:1-9 The tribe of **Simeon** inherits towns and villages within the territory of Judah in southern Canaan. Simeon was the smallest tribe entering the land according to the census figures in Num 26:12-14. Perhaps this tribe suffered heavy casualties when the Lord sent a plague upon Israel for worshiping Baal of Peor and fornicating with foreign women (the chief offender was a Simeonite, Num 25:14). See note on Num 26:12.

and Sharu'hen—thirteen cities with their villages; [7]En-rim'mon, E'ther, and A'shan—four cities with their villages; [8]together with all the villages round about these cities as far as Ba'alath-be'er, Ra'-mah of the Neg'eb. This was the inheritance of the tribe of Simeon according to its families. [9]The inheritance of the tribe of Simeon formed part of the territory of Judah; because the portion of the tribe of Judah was too large for them, the tribe of Simeon obtained an inheritance in the midst of their inheritance.

The Territory of Zebulun

10 The third lot came up for the tribe of Zeb'ulun, according to its families. And the territory of its inheritance reached as far as Sa'rid; [11]then its boundary goes up westward, and on to Mar'eal, and touches Dab'besheth, then the brook which is east of Jok'ne-am; [12]from Sa'rid it goes in the other direction eastward toward the sunrise to the boundary of Chis'loth-ta'bor; thence it goes to Dab'erath, then up to Japhi'a; [13]from there it passes along on the east toward the sunrise to Gath-he'pher, to Eth-ka'zin, and going on to Rimmon it bends toward Ne'ah; [14]then on the north the boundary turns about to Hanna'thon, and it ends at the valley of Iph'tahel; [15]and Kattath, Nahal'al, Shimron, I'dalah, and Beth-lehem—twelve cities with their villages. [16]This is the inheritance of the tribe of Zeb'ulun, according to its families—these cities with their villages.

The Territory of Issachar

17 The fourth lot came out for Is'sachar, for the tribe of Issachar, according to its families. [18]Its territory included Jezre'el, Chesul'loth, Shunem, [19]Haph'-ara-im, Shi'on, Ana'harath, [20]Rabbith, Kish'ion, E'bez, [21]Re'meth, En-gan'nim, En-had'dah, Beth-paz'-zez; [22]the boundary also touches Tabor, Shahazu'-mah, and Beth-she'mesh, and its boundary ends at the Jordan—sixteen cities with their villages. [23]This is the inheritance of the tribe of Is'sachar, according to its families—the cities with their villages.

The Territory of Asher

24 The fifth lot came out for the tribe of Asher according to its families. [25]Its territory included Helkath, Ha'li, Be'ten, Ach'shaph, [26]Allam'melech, A'mad, and Mi'shal; on the west it touches Carmel and Shihorlib'nath, [27]then it turns eastward, it goes to Beth-da'gon, and touches Zeb'ulun and the valley of Iph'tahel northward to Beth-e'mek and Nei'el; then it continues in the north to Ca'bul, [28]E'bron, Re'hob, Hammon, Kanah, as far as Sidon the Great; [29]then the boundary turns to Ra'mah, reaching to the fortified city of Tyre; then the boundary turns to Ho'sah, and it ends at the sea; Maha'lab,[p] Ach'-zib, [30]Ummah, A'phek and Re'hob—twenty-two cities with their villages. [31]This is the inheritance of the tribe of Asher according to its families—these cities with their villages.

The Territory of Naphtali

32 The sixth lot came out for the tribe of Naph'tali, for the tribe of Naphtali, according to its families. [33]And its boundary ran from He'leph, from the oak in Za-anan'nim, and Ad'ami-nek'eb, and Jab'neel, as far as Lakkum; and it ended at the Jordan; [34]then the boundary turns westward to Az'noth-ta'bor, and goes from there to Hukkok, touching Zeb'ulun at the south, and Asher on the west, and Judah on the east at the Jordan. [35]The fortified cities are Ziddim, Zer, Hammath, Rakkath, Chin'nereth, [36]Ad'amah, Ra'-mah, Ha'zor, [37]Ke'desh, Ed're-i, En-ha'zor, [38]Yi'-ron, Mig'dal-el, Horem, Beth-a'nath, and Beth-she'-mesh—nineteen cities with their villages. [39]This is the inheritance of the tribe of Naph'tali according to its families—the cities with their villages.

The Territory of Dan

40 The seventh lot came out for the tribe of Dan, according to its families. [41]And the territory of its inheritance included Zorah, Esh'ta-ol, Irshe'mesh, [42]Sha-alab'bin, Ai'jalon, Ithlah, [43]E'lon, Timnah, Ek'ron, [44]El'tekeh, Gib'bethon, Ba'alath, [45]Je'hud, Ben'e-be'rak, Gath-rim'mon, [46]and Me-jar'kon and Rakkon with the territory over against Joppa. [47]When the territory of the Da'nites was lost to them, the Danites went up and fought against Le'shem, and after capturing it and putting it to the sword they took possession of it and settled in it, calling Leshem, Dan, after the name of Dan their ancestor. [48]This is the inheritance of the tribe of Dan, according to their families—these cities with their villages.

The Inheritance of Joshua

49 When they had finished distributing the several territories of the land as inheritances, the sons of Israel gave an inheritance among them to Joshua the son of Nun. [50]By command of the LORD they gave him the city which he asked, Tim'nath-se'rah in the

---

19:47: Judg 18:27–31.

19:10–16 The tribe of **Zebulun** inherits part of lower Galilee west of the Sea of Galilee. The NT village of Nazareth lies within Zebulun's territory.

19:17–23 The tribe of **Issachar** inherits a portion of lower Galilee southwest of the Sea of Galilee. The Jezreel Valley borders it on the south.

19:24–31 The tribe of **Asher** inherits the coastland of northwest Canaan encompassing Mt. Carmel and stretching up to the city of Tyre.

19:32–39 The tribe of **Naphtali** inherits upper Galilee northwest of the Sea of Galilee.

19:40–48 The tribe of **Dan** inherits a coastal plot directly west of Benjamin. Eventually the unconquered Amorites run them out of this territory (Judg 1:34), and the tribe migrates to the far north of Canaan near the headwaters of the Jordan (19:47). For details about the Danite migration and their new settlement in Leshem (or Laish), see Judg 18:1–31.

19:50 Timnath-serah: Roughly 11 miles southwest of Shiloh, the host city of the Mosaic Tabernacle (18:1). This personal plot for Joshua will become the place of his burial (24:30).

---

[p]Cn Compare Gk: Heb *Mehebel.*

hill country of E'phraim; and he rebuilt the city, and settled in it.

51 These are the inheritances which Elea'zar the priest and Joshua the son of Nun and the heads of the fathers' houses of the tribes of the sons of Israel distributed by lot at Shiloh before the LORD, at the door of the tent of meeting. So they finished dividing the land.

The City of Refuge

20 Then the LORD said to Joshua, ²"Say to the sons of Israel, 'Appoint the cities of refuge, of which I spoke to you through Moses, ³that the manslayer who kills any person without intent or unwittingly may flee there; they shall be for you a refuge from the avenger of blood. ⁴He shall flee to one of these cities and shall stand at the entrance of the gate of the city, and explain his case to the elders of that city; then they shall take him into the city, and give him a place, and he shall remain with them. ⁵And if the avenger of blood pursues him, they shall not give up the slayer into his hand; because he killed his neighbor unwittingly, having had no enmity against him in times past. ⁶And he shall remain in that city until he has stood before the congregation for judgment, until the death of him who is high priest at the time: then the slayer may go again to his own town and his own home, to the town from which he fled.'"

7 So they set apart Ke'desh in Galilee in the hill country of Naph'tali, and She'chem in the hill country of E'phraim, and Kir'iath-ar'ba (that is, He'bron) in the hill country of Judah. ⁸And beyond the Jordan east of Jericho, they appointed Be'zer in the wilderness on the tableland, from the tribe of Reuben, and Ra'moth in Gilead, from the tribe of Gad, and Golan in Bashan, from the tribe of Manas'-seh. ⁹These were the cities designated for all the sons of Israel, and for the stranger sojourning among them, that any one who killed a person without intent could flee there, so that he might not die by the hand of the avenger of blood, till he stood before the congregation.

Cities of the Levites

21 Then the heads of the fathers' houses of the Levites came to Elea'zar the priest and to Joshua the son of Nun and to the heads of the fathers' houses of the tribes of the sons of Israel; ²and they said to them at Shiloh in the land of Canaan, "The LORD commanded through Moses that we be given cities to dwell in, along with their pasture lands for our cattle." ³So by command of the LORD the sons of Israel gave to the Levites the following cities and pasture lands out of their inheritance.

4 The lot came out for the families of the Ko'-hathites. So those Levites who were descendants of Aaron the priest received by lot from the tribes of Judah, Simeon, and Benjamin, thirteen cities.

5 And the rest of the Ko'-hathites received by lot from the families of the tribe of E'phraim, from the tribe of Dan and the half-tribe of Manas'seh, ten cities.

6 The Ger'shonites received by lot from the families of the tribe of Is'sachar, from the tribe of Asher, from the tribe of Naph'-tali, and from the half-tribe of Manas'seh in Bashan, thirteen cities.

7 The Merar'ites according to their families received from the tribe of Reuben, the tribe of Gad, and the tribe of Zeb'ulun, twelve cities.

8 These cities and their pasture lands the sons of Israel gave by lot to the Levites, as the LORD had commanded through Moses.

9 Out of the tribe of Judah and the tribe of Simeon they gave the following cities mentioned by name, ¹⁰which went to the descendants of Aaron, one of the families of the Ko'hathites who belonged to the Levites; since the lot fell to them first. ¹¹They gave them Kir'iath-ar'ba (Arba being the father of A'nak), that is He'bron, in the hill country of Judah, along with the pasture lands round about it. ¹²But the fields of the city and its villages had been given to Caleb the son of Jephun'neh as his possession.

13 And to the descendants of Aaron the priest they gave He'-bron, the city of refuge for the slayer, with its pasture lands, Libnah with its pasture lands,

---

20:2–9: Num 35:6–34; Deut 4:41–43; 19:1–13.   **21:1–42:** Num 35:1–8; 1 Chron 6:54–81.

20:1–9 Six cities of refuge are chosen to provide safe haven to manslayers. This type of protection was needed to prevent family members of the victim from hunting down and killing the manslayer without first establishing his intent (accident or murder). Three asylum cities are selected west of the Jordan (20:7) and three east of the Jordan (20:8). All six of these cities are listed among the 48 cities occupied by the Levites (21:13, 21, 27, 32, 36, 38). For background, see Num 35:9–34 and Deut 4:1–43.

20:6 high priest: His death frees the innocent manslayer to return home without fear. See note on Num 35:25.

21:1–42 The tribe of Levi inherits 48 cities dispersed throughout the tribal territories. Moses made provision for this in Num 35:1–5, when he promised the Levites places to live and property rights over adjacent grazing lands. The cities are divided among the three Levitical clans: the Kohathites

(23 cities, 21:4–5), the Gershonites (13 cities, 21:6), and the Merarites (12 cities, 21:7). It is fairly certain that lay Israelites lived alongside the Levites in these cities. Practically speaking, this meant that the clergy was spread out among the laity in order to instruct them better and minister to their needs (Lev 10:11; Deut 33:10).

21:2 Shiloh: The place of worship and solemn assembly during the settlement period. See note on 18:1.

21:4 Judah, Simeon, and Benjamin: Tribal regions that surround Jerusalem, where the Levitical priests will minister in the future Temple of Solomon.

21:10 them first: The priestly family of Aaron stands first in line among the Levitical clans to receive cities, just as the royal tribe of Judah is first among the lay tribes to receive land (15:1–61).

21:12 Caleb: Awarded parts of Hebron in 14:6–15.

¹⁴Jat'tir with its pasture lands, Eshtemo'a with its pasture lands, ¹⁵Ho'lon with its pasture lands, De'bir with its pasture lands, ¹⁶A'in with its pasture lands, Juttah with its pasture lands, Beth-she'mesh with its pasture lands—nine cities out of these two tribes; ¹⁷then out of the tribe of Benjamin, Gib'eon with its pasture lands, Ge'ba with its pasture lands, ¹⁸An'athoth with its pasture lands, and Al'mon with its pasture lands—four cities. ¹⁹The cities of the descendants of Aaron, the priests, were in all thirteen cities with their pasture lands.

20 As to the rest of the Ko'-hathites belonging to the Kohathite families of the Levites, the cities allotted to them were out of the tribe of E'phraim. ²¹To them were given She'chem, the city of refuge for the slayer, with its pasture lands in the hill country of E'phraim, Gezer with its pasture lands, ²²Kib'za-im with its pasture lands, Beth-ho'ron with its pasture lands—four cities; ²³and out of the tribe of Dan, El'teke with its pasture lands, Gib'bethon with its pasture lands, ²⁴Ai'jalon with its pasture lands, Gath-rim'mon with its pasture lands—four cities; ²⁵and out of the half-tribe of Manas'seh, Ta'anach with its pasture lands, and Gath-rim'mon with its pasture lands—two cities. ²⁶The cities of the families of the rest of the Ko'hathites were ten in all with their pasture lands.

27 And to the Ger'shonites, one of the families of the Levites, were given out of the half-tribe of Manas'seh, Golan in Bashan with its pasture lands, the city of refuge for the slayer, and Be-eshte'rah with its pasture lands—two cities; ²⁸and out of the tribe of Is'sachar, Kish'ion with its pasture lands, Dab'erath with its pasture lands, ²⁹Jarmuth with its pasture lands, En-gan'nim with its pasture lands—four cities; ³⁰and out of the tribe of Asher, Mishal with its pasture lands, Abdon with its pasture lands, ³¹Helkath with its pasture lands, and Re'hob with its pasture lands—four cities; ³²and out of the tribe of Naph'tali, Ke'desh in Galilee with its pasture lands, the city of refuge for the slayer, Ham'moth-dor with its pasture lands, and Kartan with its pasture lands—three cities. ³³The cities of the several families of the Ger'shonites were in all thirteen cities with their pasture lands.

34 And to the rest of the Levites, the Merar'ite families, were given out of the tribe of Zeb'ulun, Jok'ne-am with its pasture lands, Kartah with its pasture lands, ³⁵Dimnah with its pasture lands, Nahal'al with its pasture lands—four cities; ³⁶and out of the tribe of Reuben, Be'zer with its pasture lands, Ja'haz with its pasture lands, ³⁷Ked'emoth with its pasture lands, and Meph'a-ath with its pasture lands—four cities; ³⁸and out of the tribe of Gad, Ra'moth in Gilead with its pasture lands, the city of refuge for the slayer, Ma"hana'im with its pasture lands, ³⁹Heshbon with its pasture lands, Ja'zer with its pasture lands—four cities in all. ⁴⁰As for the cities of the several Merar'ite families, that is, the remainder of the families of the Levites, those allotted to them were in all twelve cities.

41 The cities of the Levites in the midst of the possession of the sons of Israel were in all forty-eight cities with their pasture lands. ⁴²These cities had each its pasture lands round about it; so it was with all these cities.

43 Thus the LORD gave to Israel all the land which he swore to give to their fathers; and having taken possession of it, they settled there. ⁴⁴And the LORD gave them rest on every side just as he had sworn to their fathers; not one of all their enemies had withstood them, for the LORD had given all their enemies into their hands. ⁴⁵Not one of all the good promises which the LORD had made to the house of Israel had failed; all came to pass.

The Eastern Tribes Return

22 Then Joshua summoned the Reubenites, and the Gadites, and the half-tribe of Manas'seh, ²and said to them, "You have kept all that Moses the servant of the LORD commanded you, and have obeyed my voice in all that I have commanded you; ³you have not forsaken your brethren these many days, down to this day, but have been careful to keep the charge of the LORD your God. ⁴And now the LORD your God has given rest to your brethren, as he promised them; therefore turn and go to your

---

22:1–34: 1:12–18; Num 32:20–22.

21:43–45 Briefly summarizes the theology of the Book of Joshua. Its major premise is that Yahweh has been faithful to the covenant oath he swore to the Patriarchs to make Canaan a homeland for the family of Abraham (Gen 15:18–21; 17:8). Fidelity to this pledge moved Yahweh to fight on Israel's behalf and to guarantee the success of the Conquest (10:42). See introduction: *Themes*.

21:44 rest: The initial campaigns against Canaan (chaps. 6–11) neutralize the principal enemy threats, although some parts of the land remain unconquered and other battles will need to be fought in the days ahead (13:1–7). The point is not that peacetime has begun in earnest, but that Israel has subjugated enough of the land by its united efforts to begin the process of dispersing and occupying the various tribal territories (11:23). See note on 1:13.

22:1–24:33 The final three chapters each follow the same basic outline: Joshua *summons* the people (22:1; 23:2; 24:1), reminds them of the divine *blessings* already received (22:4; 23:3–5; 24:2–12), and urges them to remain *faithful* to Yahweh and his covenant into the future (22:5–6; 23:6–16; 24:14–15).

22:1–9 The Transjordan tribes have fulfilled their obligations to fight in the national war against Canaan. Joshua commends them for this and sends them back to their territories east of the Jordan. Their agreement to serve in the campaigns west of the Jordan was accepted by Moses in Num 32:1–32 and reaffirmed by Joshua in 1:12–18.

22:4 rest: A relative cessation of conflict. See notes on 1:13 and 21:44.

home in the land where your possession lies, which Moses the servant of the LORD gave you on the other side of the Jordan. ⁵Take good care to observe the commandment and the law which Moses the servant of the LORD commanded you, to love the LORD your God, and to walk in all his ways, and to keep his commandments, and to cling to him, and to serve him with all your heart and with all your soul." ⁶So Joshua blessed them, and sent them away; and they went to their homes.

7 Now to the one half of the tribe of Manas'seh Moses had given a possession in Bashan; but to the other half Joshua had given a possession beside their brethren in the land west of the Jordan. And when Joshua sent them away to their homes and blessed them, ⁸he said to them, "Go back to your homes with much wealth, and with very many cattle, with silver, gold, bronze, and iron, and with much clothing; divide the spoil of your enemies with your brethren." ⁹So the Reubenites and the Gadites and the half-tribe of Manas'seh returned home, parting from the sons of Israel at Shiloh, which is in the land of Canaan, to go to the land of Gilead, their own land of which they had possessed themselves by command of the LORD through Moses.

An Altar of Witness by the Jordan

10 And when they came to the region about the Jordan, that lies in the land of Canaan, the Reubenites and the Gadites and the half-tribe of Manas'seh built there an altar by the Jordan, an altar of great size. ¹¹And the sons of Israel heard say, "Behold, the Reubenites and the Gadites and the half-tribe of Manas'seh have built an altar at the frontier of the land of Canaan, in the region about the Jordan, on the side that belongs to the sons of Israel." ¹²And when the sons of Israel heard of it, the whole assembly of the sons of Israel gathered at Shiloh, to make war against them.

13 Then the sons of Israel sent to the Reubenites and the Gadites and the half-tribe of Manas'seh, in the land of Gilead, Phin'ehas the son of Elea'zar the priest, ¹⁴and with him ten chiefs, one from each of the tribal families of Israel, every one of them the head of a family among the clans of Israel. ¹⁵And they came to the Reubenites, the Gadites, and the half-tribe of Manas'seh, in the land of Gilead, and they said to them, ¹⁶"Thus says the whole congregation of the LORD, 'What is this treachery which you have committed against the God of Israel in turning away this day from following the LORD, by building yourselves an altar this day in rebellion against the LORD? ¹⁷Have we not had enough of the sin at Peor from which even yet we have not cleansed ourselves, and for which there came a plague upon the congregation of the LORD, ¹⁸that you must turn away this day from following the LORD? And if you rebel against the LORD today he will be angry with the whole congregation of Israel tomorrow. ¹⁹But now, if your land is unclean, pass over into the LORD's land where the LORD's tabernacle stands, and take for yourselves a possession among us; only do not rebel against the LORD, or make us as rebels by building yourselves an altar other than the altar of the LORD our God. ²⁰Did not A'chan the son of Ze'rah break faith in the matter of the devoted things, and wrath fell upon all the congregation of Israel? And he did not perish alone for his iniquity.'"

21 Then the Reubenites, the Gadites, and the half-tribe of Manas'seh said in answer to the heads of the families of Israel, ²²"The Mighty One, God, the LORD! The Mighty One, God, the LORD! He knows; and let Israel itself know! If it was in rebellion or in breach of faith toward the LORD, spare us not today ²³for building an altar to turn away from following the LORD; or if we did so to offer burnt offerings or cereal offerings or peace offerings on it, may the LORD himself take vengeance. ²⁴No, but we did it from fear that in time to come your children might say to our children, 'What have you to do with the LORD, the God of Israel? ²⁵For the LORD has made the Jordan a boundary between us and you, you Reubenites and

---

22:7 Bashan: The land east of the Sea of Galilee.

22:9 Shiloh: The place of worship and solemn assembly during the settlement period. See note on 18:1. **Gilead:** The central region of the Transjordan, directly east of the river.

22:10–34 The Transjordan tribes instigate a temporary crisis when they build a giant altar on the Jordan riverbank. The tribes west of the Jordan interpret this as an act of treachery and rebellion (22:16), as though Reuben, Gad, and half-Manasseh were building a rival sanctuary in competition with the Tabernacle of the Lord (22:19) already set up in Shiloh (18:1). War is averted when the purpose of the altar is discovered: it was designed, not for public worship, but as a monument to the common faith that unites the tribes of Israel living on both sides of the Jordan (22:21–29).

22:10 in the land: Suggests the altar was erected on the west bank of the Jordan, which is in the land of Canaan proper (Num 33:51). Some scholars interpret 22:11 to mean the altar stood on the east bank, facing Canaan but technically outside it.

22:13 Phinehas: Grandson of Aaron who stands next in line to receive the high priesthood from his father, Eleazar (Ex 6:23–25). He is here a member of the western delegation sent to investigate the motives of the eastern tribes for erecting the altar.

22:17 sin at Peor: Refers to the apostasy of the Conquest generation just before entering the land (Num 25:1–5). Phinehas, the spokesman for the delegation, remembers this well, for he had the courage to intervene and take action against the Peor rebellion (Num 25:6–13; Ps 106:28–31).

22:19 the LORD's land: Designates the "land of Canaan" west of the Jordan but seems to exclude the "land of Gilead" east of the Jordan (22:9). That the Promised Land is ultimately Yahweh's possession, see Lev 25:23.

22:20 did not perish alone: The Achan affair in Josh 7 exemplifies how the sin of one can affect the entire covenant community. See note on 7:25.

22:22 Mighty One, God, the LORD!: Divine names are invoked to summon Yahweh as a witness to the innocent intentions of Reuben, Gad, and Manasseh.

Gadites; you have no portion in the LORD.' So your children might make our children cease to worship the LORD. ²⁶Therefore we said, 'Let us now build an altar, not for burnt offering, nor for sacrifice, ²⁷but to be a witness between us and you, and between the generations after us, that we do perform the service of the LORD in his presence with our burnt offerings and sacrifices and peace offerings; lest your children say to our children in time to come, "You have no portion in the LORD."' ²⁸And we thought, If this should be said to us or to our descendants in time to come, we should say, 'Behold the copy of the altar of the LORD, which our fathers made, not for burnt offerings, nor for sacrifice, but to be a witness between us and you.' ²⁹Far be it from us that we should rebel against the LORD, and turn away this day from following the LORD by building an altar for burnt offering, cereal offering, or sacrifice, other than the altar of the LORD our God that stands before his tabernacle!"

30 When Phin'ehas the priest and the chiefs of the congregation, the heads of the families of Israel who were with him, heard the words that the Reubenites and the Gadites and the Manas'sites spoke, it pleased them well. ³¹And Phin'ehas the son of Elea'zar the priest said to the Reubenites and the Gadites and the Manas'sites, "Today we know that the LORD is in the midst of us, because you have not committed this treachery against the LORD; now you have saved the sons of Israel from the hand of the LORD."

32 Then Phin'ehas the son of Elea'zar the priest, and the chiefs, returned from the Reubenites and the Gadites in the land of Gilead to the land of Canaan, to the sons of Israel, and brought back word to them. ³³And the report pleased the sons of Israel; and the sons of Israel blessed God and spoke no more of making war against them, to destroy the land where the Reubenites and the Gadites were settled. ³⁴The Reubenites and the Gadites called the altar Witness; "For," said they, "it is a witness between us that the LORD is God."

Joshua Exhorts the People

23 A long time afterward, when the LORD had given rest to Israel from all their enemies round about, and Joshua was old and well advanced in years, ²Joshua summoned all Israel, their elders and heads, their judges and officers, and said to them, "I am now old and well advanced in years; ³and you have seen all that the LORD your God has done to all these nations for your sake, for it is the LORD your God who has fought for you. ⁴Behold, I have allotted to you as an inheritance for your tribes those nations that remain, along with all the nations that I have already cut off, from the Jordan to the Great Sea in the west. ⁵The LORD your God will push them back before you, and drive them out of your sight; and you shall possess their land, as the LORD your God promised you. ⁶Therefore be very steadfast to keep and do all that is written in the book of the law of Moses, turning aside from it neither to the right hand nor to the left, ⁷that you may not be mixed with these nations left here among you, or make mention of the names of their gods, or swear by them, or serve them, or bow down yourselves to them, ⁸but cling to the LORD your God as you have done to this day. ⁹For the LORD has driven out before you great and strong nations; and as for you, no man has been able to withstand you to this day. ¹⁰One man of you puts to flight a thousand, since it is the LORD your God who fights for you, as he promised you. ¹¹Take good heed to yourselves, therefore, to love the LORD your God. ¹²For if you turn back, and join the remnant of these nations left here among you, and make marriages with them, so that you marry their women and they yours, ¹³know assuredly that the LORD your God will not continue to drive out these nations before you; but they shall be a snare and a trap for you, a scourge on your sides, and thorns in your eyes, till you perish from off this good land which the LORD your God has given you.

14 "And now I am about to go the way of all the earth, and you know in your hearts and souls,

---

22:31 saved the sons of Israel: Rescued from certain judgment, had the altar of witness been intended for unlawful liturgies.

23:1-16 Joshua delivers a farewell sermon to the leaders of Israel. Deuteronomic in style, it is similar to the parting exhortations of Moses (Deut 31:1-29), Samuel (1 Sam 12:1-25), and David (1 Kings 2:1-9).

23:1 rest: Regional peace is a provisional fulfillment of Deut 12:10. However, the complete realization of this promise awaits the time of King David (2 Sam 7:1). For the meaning of "rest" in Joshua, see note on 21:44.

23:2 all Israel: Not every single Israelite, but leaders of Israel representing every single tribe (24:1). Presumably this gathering takes place in Shiloh where the Tabernacle stands (18:1).

23:3 fought for you: For Yahweh as a divine Warrior, see introduction: *Themes*.

23:4 nations that remain: Peoples and territories still unconquered (13:1-7). **the Great Sea:** The Mediterranean.

23:6 the book of the law: The Book of Deuteronomy, which Moses wrote on a scroll and placed "by the side of" the Ark of the Covenant, according to Deut 31:26.

23:7 not be mixed: The covenant between Yahweh and Israel is sacred and exclusive. This means that Israel is forbidden to make alliances with foreign peoples in their midst or to intermarry with the surviving Canaanites; rather, it must eliminate them from the land and destroy every last trace of their idolatrous cults. Assimilating pagan ways will bring painful consequences and lead eventually to exile from the land (23:13). This uncompromising policy of separation is noted several times in the Torah (Ex 23:32-33; 34:12-16; Lev 18:3; Deut 7:1-5).

23:14 go the way of all: An idiom meaning that Joshua is nearing death (1 Kings 2:1-2). He was 110 years old when he died (24:29).

all of you, that not one thing has failed of all the good things which the Lord your God promised concerning you; all have come to pass for you, not one of them has failed. ¹⁵But just as all the good things which the Lord your God promised concerning you have been fulfilled for you, so the Lord will bring upon you all the evil things, until he has destroyed you from off this good land which the Lord your God has given you, ¹⁶if you transgress the covenant of the Lord your God, which he commanded you, and go and serve other gods and bow down to them. Then the anger of the Lord will be kindled against you, and you shall perish quickly from off the good land which he has given to you."

The Tribes Renew the Covenant

24 *Then Joshua gathered all the tribes of Israel to She'chem, and summoned the elders, the heads, the judges, and the officers of Israel; and they presented themselves before God. ²And Joshua said to all the people, "Thus says the Lord, the God of Israel, 'Your fathers lived of old beyond the Euphrates, Te'rah, the father of Abraham and of Na'hor; and they served other gods. ³Then I took your father Abraham from beyond the River and led him through all the land of Canaan, and made his offspring many. I gave him Isaac; ⁴and to Isaac I gave Jacob and Esau. And I gave Esau the hill country of Se'ir to possess, but Jacob and his children went down to Egypt. ⁵And I sent Moses and Aaron, and I plagued Egypt with what I did in the midst of it; and afterwards I brought you out. ⁶Then I brought your fathers out of Egypt, and you came to the sea; and the Egyptians pursued

your fathers with chariots and horsemen to the Red Sea. ⁷And when they cried to the Lord, he put darkness between you and the Egyptians, and made the sea come upon them and cover them; and your eyes saw what I did to Egypt; and you lived in the wilderness a long time. ⁸Then I brought you to the land of the Am'orites, who lived on the other side of the Jordan; they fought with you, and I gave them into your hand, and you took possession of their land, and I destroyed them before you. ⁹Then Balak the son of Zippor, king of Moab, arose and fought against Israel; and he sent and invited Balaam the son of Beor to curse you, ¹⁰but I would not listen to Balaam; therefore he blessed you; so I delivered you out of his hand. ¹¹And you went over the Jordan and came to Jericho, and the men of Jericho fought against you, and also the Am'orites, the Per'izzites, the Canaanites, the Hittites, the Gir'gashites, the Hi'vites, and the Jeb'usites; and I gave them into your hand. ¹²And I sent the hornet before you, which drove them out before you, the two kings of the Am'orites; it was not by your sword or by your bow. ¹³I gave you a land on which you had not labored, and cities which you had not built, and you dwell therein; you eat the fruit of vineyards and oliveyards which you did not plant.'

14 "Now therefore fear the Lord, and serve him in sincerity and in faithfulness; put away the gods which your fathers served beyond the River, and in Egypt, and serve the Lord. ¹⁵And if you be unwilling to serve the Lord, choose this day whom you will serve, whether the gods your fathers served in the region beyond the River, or the gods of the

---

23:15 good things: The blessings of the Deuteronomic covenant detailed in Deut 28:1-14. **evil things:** The curses of the Deuteronomic covenant spelled out in Deut 28:15-68.

24:1-28 Joshua assembles Israel at Shechem to *renew* the Deuteronomic covenant, just as he assembled Israel at Shechem some 30 years earlier to *ratify* the Deuteronomic covenant (8:30-35) as Moses prescribed before his death (Deut 27:1-14). The event is a summons for the next generation, destined to outlive Joshua, to renounce other gods and to pledge their exclusive allegiance to Yahweh (24:23). Renewal ceremonies were a common feature of ancient Near Eastern treaty covenants (the Deuteronomic covenant was no exception, Deut 31:10-13).

24:1 Shechem: A city in central Palestine in the territory of Manasseh (17:1-2). It sits in the shadow of two mountain peaks, Mount Ebal on its north side and Mount Gerizim on its south side. The Greek LXX reads "Shiloh" instead of "Shechem" in 24:1 and 24:25. **before God:** Perhaps indicates that the Tabernacle was moved to Shechem for the occasion (also 24:26). It had been stationed in Shiloh (18:1).

24:2-13 Joshua rehearses the early history of Israel. He starts with the call of Abraham (24:3), touches on the Exodus (24:5), the wilderness period (24:7), and the seizure of the Transjordan (24:8), and ends with the Conquest of Canaan

(24:11). The focus throughout is on the gracious actions of God (note the repetition of the divine "I").

24:2 beyond the Euphrates: Abraham hails from Ur in lower Mesopotamia (Gen 11:27-31). Being people of their times, his family shared the Near Eastern belief in many gods.

24:4 country of Seir: The land of Edom, south of the Dead Sea (Gen 32:3; Deut 2:5).

24:9 Balaam: Hired by the Moabites to curse the camp of Israel before the start of the Conquest. See note on Num 22:5.

24:12 hornet: Symbolizes the divine power sent to terrify the Canaanites and run them out of the Promised Land (Ex 23:28; Deut 7:20). **not by your sword:** Victory in battle is an act of Yahweh, not a human achievement about which Israel could boast (Ps 44:3-8).

24:13 you had not built: Israel's occupation of Canaanite towns and homesteads fulfills the promise of Moses in Deut 6:10-11. It implies that Joshua's army did not level and burn the physical structures of every settlement it conquered. Demolition and fire were only required for three cities: Jericho (6:24), Ai (8:28), and Hazor (11:13).

24:14 fear the Lord: The beginning of wisdom and responsible living (Prov 1:7). Genuine fear of Yahweh is a deterrent from sin (Ex 20:20; Job 1:1). **in Egypt:** Israel's attachment to the idols of Egypt is not mentioned explicitly in Exodus but is brought out in Ezekiel (Ezek 20:7-8; 23:3, 8, 19-21).

24:15 choose this day: The covenant involves a free decision to serve Yahweh or foreign gods. One choice brings the blessing of prosperity and life, the other a curse of adversity and death (Deut 11:26-28; 30:15-18).

---

*24:1: The full gathering of the tribes at Shechem for a renewal of the covenant sealed the conquest and the final apportioning of the land. It seems to indicate the conversion to the worship of Yahweh of those Hebrews who did not go down to Egypt.

Am′orites in whose land you dwell; but as for me and my house, we will serve the LORD."

16 Then the people answered, "Far be it from us that we should forsake the LORD, to serve other gods; [17]for it is the LORD our God who brought us and our fathers up from the land of Egypt, out of the house of bondage, and who did those great signs in our sight, and preserved us in all the way that we went, and among all the peoples through whom we passed; [18]and the LORD drove out before us all the peoples, the Am′orites who lived in the land; therefore we also will serve the LORD, for he is our God."

19 But Joshua said to the people, "You cannot serve the LORD; for he is a holy God; he is a jealous God; he will not forgive your transgressions or your sins. [20]If you forsake the LORD and serve foreign gods, then he will turn and do you harm, and consume you, after having done you good." [21]And the people said to Joshua, "No; but we will serve the LORD." [22]Then Joshua said to the people, "You are witnesses against yourselves that you have chosen the LORD, to serve him." And they said, "We are witnesses." [23]He said, "Then put away the foreign gods which are among you, and incline your heart to the LORD, the God of Israel." [24]And the people said to Joshua, "The LORD our God we will serve, and his voice we will obey." [25]So Joshua made a covenant with the people that day, and made statutes and ordinances for them at She′chem. [26]And Joshua wrote these words in the book of the law of God; and he took a great stone, and set it up there under the oak in the sanctuary of the LORD. [27]And Joshua said to all the people, "Behold, this stone shall be a witness against us; for it has heard all the words of the LORD which he spoke to us; therefore it shall be a witness against you, lest you deal falsely with your God." [28]So Joshua sent the people away, every man to his inheritance.

The Death of Joshua and Eleazar

29 After these things Joshua the son of Nun, the servant of the LORD, died, being a hundred and ten years old. [30]And they buried him in his own inheritance at Tim′nath-se′rah, which is in the hill country of E′phraim, north of the mountain of Ga′ash.

31 And Israel served the LORD all the days of Joshua, and all the days of the elders who outlived Joshua and had known all the work which the LORD did for Israel.

32 The bones of Joseph which the sons of Israel brought up from Egypt were buried at She′chem, in the portion of ground which Jacob bought from the sons of Ha′mor the father of She′chem for a hundred pieces of money;[q] it became an inheritance of the descendants of Joseph.

33 And Elea′zar the son of Aaron died; and they buried him at Gib′e-ah, the town of Phin′ehas his son, which had been given him in the hill country of E′phraim.

24:32: Gen 50:24, 25; Ex 13:19; Acts 7:16.

24:19 You cannot serve: The RSV translation renders this as a *prophecy* of Israel's future failings (like the one given by Moses, Deut 30:1). Others read it as a *warning* against overconfidence in the face of Yahweh's high and difficult standards ("You may not be able to serve").

24:23 put away the foreign gods: Joshua's summons to renounce idols at Shechem evokes memories of Jacob urging his caravan to dispose of foreign gods at Shechem in Gen 35:1–4 (CCC 2113).

24:25 made a covenant: I.e., renewed the Deuteronomic covenant. See note on 24:1–28.

24:26 under the oak: Possibly the "oak of Moreh", where Abraham built the first altar to Yahweh in the land of Canaan (Gen 12:6–7). Likewise, this may be the place where Jacob buried the Mesopotamian idols that were discarded in Shechem (Gen 35:4).

24:27 this stone: A boulder turned up on end as a memorial. It stands as a witness to the covenant commitment being made by Israel. This is the eighth and final stone monument in Joshua that bears witness to the Conquest of the land and the covenant between Yahweh and Israel (4:9, 20; 7:26; 8:29,

32; 10:27; 22:26–27). For other pillars erected in covenant ceremonies, see Gen 31:44–45, Ex 24:4; and Deut 27:2. **witness:** Invoking witnesses was a standard feature of Near Eastern covenant procedure, as also reflected in Deuteronomy (Deut 30:19; 31:19, 26).

24:29–33 The death of Joshua (24:29) and Eleazar (24:33) closes out the Conquest period, just as the death of their predecessors, Moses and Aaron, closed out the Exodus period (Num 20:28; Deut 34:5). Joshua and Eleazar are both buried in the hill country of Ephraim (24:30, 33).

24:29 servant of the LORD: At the end of his life, Joshua is honored with the same title that was given to Moses throughout the book (1:1, 13; 8:31, 33; 11:12, etc.). For other parallels between the two leaders, see note on 1:5.

24:30 Timnath-serah: Joshua's hometown in Ephraimite territory. See note on 19:50.

24:32 bones of Joseph: The patriarch was mummified in Egypt (Gen 50:26), his remains were carried out of Egypt at the time of the Exodus (Ex 13:19), and now his body is laid to rest in Shechem, in the territory belonging to Manasseh, his first-born son (17:1-2). **Jacob bought:** The purchase was made in Gen 33:19.

24:33 Eleazar: Son and successor of Aaron, the first high priest of Israel (Num 20:25-28; Deut 10:6).

---

[q]Heb *qesitah*.

STUDY QUESTIONS
Joshua

Chapter 1

For understanding
1. **1:1.** At what point does the Book of Joshua begin? Who has the honorary title "servant of the Lord"? What has Joshua accomplished together with Caleb? Allegorically, according to St. Jerome, how is Joshua a type of the Lord Jesus? According to Lactantius, why does Joshua succeed Moses?
2. **1:4.** How large is the land promised to Israel supposed to be in comparison with the land conquered under Joshua? When does it come under Israelite control?
3. **1:5.** With what is Joshua graced? What are the nine explicit statements and implicit suggestions that highlight the similarities between Joshua and his forebear Moses?
4. **1:13.** When will Israel enjoy the Lord's peace and protection in Canaan? What will this new era follow? In the Book of Hebrews, of what is the *rest* that Joshua gives the people in Canaan a sign?

For application
1. **1:1–2.** Has the death or departure of a leader ever left you feeling uneasy about the future? Did new responsibilities fall upon you because that person was gone? If so, what considerations helped you to assume your new responsibilities?
2. **1:5.** Scripture promises that the Lord will not fail or forsake those who seek him (Ps 9:10; 37:28; 94:14; Is 41:17). How confident are you of such promises for yourself? Have you ever called on the Lord for help and received it? If so, how did that assistance affect your overall confidence?
3. **1:7.** The Lord exhorts Joshua not to turn from the Law "to the right hand or to the left"—in other words, to be strict in his obedience to it. What are some temptations to swerve from the moral law that people in our culture face by relaxing their obedience to it? Why is being strict with yourself generally better than letting yourself off easy when it comes to moral choices?
4. **1:13.** The note for this verse refers to Heb 4:1–10, which stresses faith and obedience, and says (in part) that "we who have believed enter into that rest." About what kind of rest is Hebrews talking? What does Hebrews (quoting Ps 95) mean by exhorting us to listen to the Lord's voice today?

Chapter 2

For understanding
1. **2:1–24.** Where is ancient Jericho located? How was it built? As one of the oldest settlements known to history, how long has Jericho been inhabited? What have archaeological excavations at Jericho unearthed? About what do experts disagree regarding Jericho's demise? What complicates the interpretation of the evidence?
2. **2:1.** What is Shittim, and where is it located? Although the Hebrew refers to a "prostitute", what does Jewish tradition consider Rahab to be? As a Canaanite, what shows her conversion to the faith of Israel? How does she escape the devastation of Jericho? As what does the NT designate Rahab? Allegorically, according to Cassiodorus, of what is Rahab a type?
3. **2:15.** What have archeologists discovered above the lower revetment wall around Jericho? How would one escape the city once the gates had been closed for the night? How is this similar to Paul's escape from Damascus?
4. **2:18.** Of what is the scarlet cord a sign? Allegorically, according to St. Jerome, what does the color of the cord signify, and of what is Rahab a type? How does St. Justin Martyr understand the red cord?

For application
1. **2:5.** Read the note for this verse, particularly the part about lying. Why is lying an evil act? How is lying an offense against justice and charity (CCC 2485)? If you were in a hostile situation that required you to witness to your faith, how should you profess it (cf. CCC 2471)?
2. **2:11.** This verse is where Rahab professes her belief in "the Lᴏʀᴅ your God", on the basis of what she has heard he has done. What is the basis of *your* faith in God? Through what process did you come to that faith?
3. **2:18.** Several sacramentals, such as certain scapulars and medals, have promises attached to them related to preserving people in the state of grace. What prevents these from becoming magical or idolatrous talismans? What is the purpose of sacramentals like these in their holders' lives?
4. **2:24.** Why do you think the culture of the world is so hostile to Christianity? What does the world's hostility say about the power of the Christian message? How should that power encourage you as someone commissioned by your Baptism to proclaim it?

Chapter 3

For understanding
1. **3:1—5:1.** What do these chapters describe? What are five ways in which the narrative is worded to evoke memories of the Exodus? Morally, according to St. Gregory of Nyssa, what does the crossing of the Jordan teach us to do?
2. **3:3.** What does the Ark of the Covenant represent? What does the prominent role of the Ark in Joshua show?
3. **3:15.** Why does the Jordan overflow? What does stressing the high water level do in the story? When does the time of harvest begin?
4. **3:16.** Where is the town of Adam? Where is the Salt Sea in relation to the town? Although how the Lord effected the damming of the Jordan is not described, to what do medieval and modern reports attest? Allegorically, according to Origen, how does the crossing of the Jordan serve as a type of Baptism?

Study Questions

For application

1. **3:3–4.** The text says that the Israelites must not come near the Ark of the Covenant out of respect for the awesome presence and power of God. How near does God want you to come to him? How do you express reverence for his presence in the Most Blessed Sacrament? In what ways might you be overly casual in your handling of sacred things (such as the Bible)?
2. **3:5.** Read the note for this verse. How might the actions mentioned there suggest an interior purification? If you were told to sanctify yourself before coming to Mass this Sunday, what would you do?
3. **3:10.** Joshua proclaims that God is a living God. What does Jesus mean by claiming that he is life itself (Jn 11:25; 14:6)? How does he communicate this life to you (e.g., Jn 3:15; 4:14; 6:35, 47–48)?

Chapter 4

For understanding

1. **4:3.** What do the twelve stones represent? Where are they carried, and why? What wordplay might the author intend with the Hebrew word for "stone"? Allegorically, according to St. Gregory of Nyssa, of what are the twelve stones set up at the Jordan a type?
2. **4:7.** How many stone monuments are set up in Canaan, and to what do they bear witness?
3. **4:19.** What is the first month of the Hebrew calendar, and when does it start? What happens on the tenth of Abib? What does the name Gilgal mean? Where is it located, and what purpose does it serve for Joshua?
4. **4:24.** What is the purpose of divine miracles? What function does news of the Lord's mighty acts serve?

For application

1. **4:5–7.** What souvenirs have you collected over the years, and what do they mean to you? How many of them are souvenirs that remind you of your faith (e.g., souvenirs of a pilgrimage)? How might they help you to communicate your faith to your children or other relatives?
2. **4:9.** Certain shrines, such as the one at Lourdes, display items that visitors leave there, such as crutches or braces. Why are they there? What do they mean to the people who left them and to those who see them afterward?
3. **4:19.** The note for this verse points out the link between the timing of the Jordan crossing and the date when lambs were selected for the first Passover. What is the liturgical significance behind the timing of Easter with Passover or between the descent of the Holy Spirit on the apostles and the Jewish feast of Pentecost? Why do people often time an important event, such as a wedding, so that it occurs on the anniversary of another important family event?

Chapter 5

For understanding

1. **5:1–12.** With what two liturgical events does Israel's life in Canaan begin? Of what is circumcision the sign? What does Passover commemorate? What is the reason for completing these two events at this point?
2. **5:2.** How does the way flint fractures determine the use of these knives? Why is it important before Passover to circumcise males born during the wilderness wandering? Allegorically, according to Tertullian, why does Joshua instead of Moses lead a new people into Canaan, and what does this have to do with Jesus? According to Lactantius, how does the second circumcision go beyond the first?
3. **5:9.** How could the events of the Exodus put Yahweh's reputation on the line? What play on words is the author making about Gilgal?
4. **5:12.** How does Yahweh feed Israel for 40 years of wilderness wandering? Of what did its flavor offer a foretaste? What does the end of the manna signal?

For application

1. **5:1–12.** The note for these verses says that circumcision and the celebration of Passover prepare Israel for coming battles. How can Christians prepare themselves for the spiritual battles that they will face? What benefits do regular reception of Penance and the Eucharist provide in this regard?
2. **5:2–7.** According to CCC 1257, why is Baptism necessary for entrance into the Communion of Saints? What is the responsibility of Christian parents to have their children baptized? What is their responsibility after Baptism has taken place?
3. **5:11–12.** How have the personal and spiritual supports you enjoyed as a child changed now that you are an adult? Which (if any) of these supports have continued into adulthood, and which changes have forced you to take responsibility for yourself and others?
4. **5:15.** The angel tells Joshua to take his sandals off, as Moses did, "for the place where you stand is holy". What benefit is there for Joshua in direct physical contact with the holy (without the interference of his sandals)? With what holy things do you have direct physical contact? What benefit does such contact confer on you?

Chapter 6

For understanding

1. **6:1–27.** As the lead character in the story of the conquest of Jericho, what does Yahweh do? In these events, what do we see of the Lord's activity? Anagogically, according to Origen, what does the fall of Jericho prefigure? According to St. Augustine, what happens when the walls of Jericho (representing the frail defenses of the world) fall?
2. **6:4.** What does the number seven enumerate? Since in Hebrew the word seven (*sheba'*) shares the same root as the verb for swearing an oath (*shaba'*), what may the number signal? How does the second wave of judgments in the Book of Revelation evoke memories of the fall of Jericho? According to St. Cyril of Jerusalem, how does the fall of the walls of Jericho resemble the destruction of the Jewish Temple in Jerusalem?
3. **Word Study: Devoted (6:17).** What does the Hebrew word *ḥerem* mean? What things can be devoted in this sense? In the context of Israelite warfare, how are persons and things dedicated to Yahweh, and how does Jericho serve as an example?

What happens to warriors who violate the ban on devoted things by taking what is forbidden? On which cities and towns is the ban placed? Historically, where else besides Israel is the law of the ban attested to?

4. **Essay: The Conquest of Canaan.** What reaction do many readers have when they read the war stories of the Book of Joshua? Before all else, what is the purpose of the war against Canaan, and how does Scripture reveal this underlying reason? How is the Conquest also a form of divine protection of Israel, and how does Scripture highlight that aspect? Despite common misperceptions, how is the Israelite Conquest of Canaan *not* a form of ethnic cleansing, and what are some ways in which that is made clear?

For application

1. **6:4–5.** Read the note for v. 4. Since the trumpet is used as a call to worship as well as to battle (e.g., Num 29:1; Is 27:13), how are worship and spiritual warfare interrelated?
2. **6:8.** What purposes do public religious processions, like Corpus Christi processions, serve? How might such events resemble the procession of Israelites around Jericho?
3. **6:12–16.** While the tactic of an army repeatedly circling the city in silence (except for the blowing of trumpets) for a week would inspire fear in the citizens of Jericho, what would it do for the soldiers in Joshua's army? In a similar vein, why would a Christian choose to repeat a set of formal prayers over a set period of time (e.g., like the nine First Fridays)? Why is such persistent prayer important?
4. **6:17–18.** Read the word study note for v. 17. For Christians, how would an application of the "ban" involve ridding ourselves of anything that leads us into sin, such as putting aside possessions, pastimes, even questionable friends? What has the "banning" of such things meant to you in your pursuit of holiness?

Chapter 7

For understanding

1. **7:1.** How does Israel break faith with Yahweh? Who is the culprit? How is his thievery a double violation of the ban?
2. **7:2.** What does the name Ai mean? Where is the town located? Where has archaeology located it, and why is the identification problematic? Where (or what) is Beth-aven?
3. **7:25.** Because it is difficult to understand why the family of Achan shares the fate of the criminal himself, what three considerations may help explain it?
4. **7:26.** How is Achan's body buried? Against what is this crude memorial a warning? What is the significance of the name Valley of Achor? How does the prophet Hosea, looking to a future age, envision the place?

For application

1. **7:4–5.** How do small setbacks in your spiritual life, such as falling into old patterns of sin, affect your confidence in God? What is usually their cause? What approach do you take toward a remedy?
2. **7:6–9.** The second of the Beatitudes is "Blessed are those who mourn, for they shall be comforted" (Mt 5:4). What are some of Joshua's reasons for mourning over the sin of Israel? Why does Jesus consider those who grieve over sin to be blessed? Why do many Christians fail to mourn over sin (their own or that of others) when the results are often so clearly disastrous?
3. **7:12a.** How does the commission of even a single venial sin weaken a person? According to CCC 1863, what does venial sin weaken, even though it does not deprive the sinner of sanctifying grace? How does sin do that?
4. **7:24–25.** Why is there no such thing as a totally private sin? How does my sin affect my family, my friends, and my community, even if they are not guilty of it?

Chapter 8

For understanding

1. **8:1–29.** How is the conquest of Ai accomplished? What happens to the king of Ai and his servicemen and civilians as a result?
2. **8:2.** Why is booty allowed at Ai? Although Ai and its inhabitants would normally fall under the ban, of what do the spoils consist? Of what does the relaxation of the ban for Ai appear to be an instance?
3. **8:18.** What does Joshua's battlefield gesture with the javelin signify? How does it resemble what Moses did during the battle with the Amalekites?
4. **8:30–35.** How do the priests and the lay tribes participate in the public ratification of the Deuteronomic covenant? Where does the ceremony take place? Why is the location significant?

For application

1. **8:2.** As circumstances change, the Church may relax certain regulations, such as the length of the Communion fast or the former Lenten disciplines. What considerations might prompt the Church to relax the rules? How might relaxing the rules change the attitudes of the faithful toward practices of self-discipline or mortification?
2. **8:16–17.** Ai's response to Israel shows how a rash offense may become the worst defense. How often, when you took what seemed like a safe initiative (like buying an expensive car or house), have you been surprised by attacks from an unexpected quarter (like a downturn in the economy)? How do such situations apply to the spiritual life (e.g., committing yourself to a cause)?
3. **8:18.** As the note for this verse indicates, Joshua's gesture represents a form of continuous intercession during battle. What kinds of battles is the Church facing nowadays? Even though Jesus promises ultimate victory, why is ongoing prayer needed? What does it do for the combatants? for the person interceding?
4. **8:30–35.** Read Deut 27 after reading these verses. How does the chapter aid your understanding of what is going on? Why are such elaborate ratification ceremonies necessary? What analogous ceremonies can you think of in Catholic Church worship? Why, for example, does the Church ask you to profess your faith after several long readings at the Easter Vigil?

Study Questions

Chapter 9

For understanding
1. **9:1-2.** How do local Canaanites respond to Israel's advance? What success will the coalition have?
2. **9:14.** To what does failure to discern the Lord's will lead? What is the consequence of the very act of making a covenant with the Gibeonites? Instead of rushing through negotiations, what should Israel have done?
3. **9:15.** How does Israel ratify a covenant of nonaggression with Gibeon? What does the treaty obligate Israel, the superior partner, to do? When will the binding force of this covenant become apparent? What may the literal expression "cut a covenant" indicate about the ceremony?
4. **9:27.** To what does "the place" refer? Where is the sanctuary stationed in Joshua's day and, then, later?

For application
1. **9:3-13.** Since their lives are at stake, the residents of Gibeon resort to subterfuge to protect themselves, and it works. What do you think of the morality of their method? To what lengths would you go to preserve your own life or that of your family? What ethical or moral considerations would guide your thinking here?
2. **9:14.** When have you or someone you know made a major decision without praying about it first? In what ways was the decision rash or precipitate? What were the consequences for those involved? What did you learn from it?
3. **9:18.** Why does Scripture condemn murmuring on the part of the People of God against their leaders (e.g., Ex 16:8; Num 14:27; Ps 106:24-27)? How justifiable in this case is the complaint of the Israelites? If you have cause for complaint against a Church leader such as a priest or a bishop, how should you make your concerns known without such "murmuring"?
4. **9:19-20.** What happened in the Catholic Church in America when, three years after the Second Vatican Council, the pope published an encyclical upholding the teaching about contraception? What should have been the response of the faithful (cf. CCC 2037-2040)? What moral dangers accompany dissent from unpopular teaching?

Chapter 10

For understanding
1. **10:1-43.** Where is Joshua's campaign taking place? Coupled with the overthrow of Jericho, Ai, and Bethel, as well as the subjugation of Gibeon, what do these military expeditions accomplish? Nevertheless, what is left for future generations to do? How does the nature of the warfare switch in chaps. 10-11?
2. **10:6.** What does the peace treaty made in 9:15 obligate Israel to do? What does the appeal for help made to Joshua mean he must do?
3. **10:13.** What does Joshua's prayer call forth? In what two ways can the poetic fragment be interpreted, and what considerations must be taken into account in either case? Whether the miracle was in the sky or on the ground, what is the only real explanation for it? What is the Book of Jashar?
4. **10:40-42.** What are these verses about? What have comparative studies of Near Eastern war annals shown about these types of synopsis statements? Taken literally, what does it sound like Israel has accomplished? However, what would ancient readers of Joshua have understood about this convention, and how is this confirmed? What does Catholic teaching hold about the interpretation of Scripture?

For application
1. **10:6-7.** If Joshua had been so inclined, how might he have excused himself from helping the Gibeonites who tricked him into a covenant? What kind of man does he show himself to be by keeping his commitment? What does his example say to those who want to avoid inconvenient responsibilities?
2. **10:13.** Miracle stories like the one narrated here often arouse a great deal of skepticism from modern readers. How do you react to stories like this? How helpful are explanations like the note for this verse? What purposes are such stories intended to serve?
3. **10:14.** Of the three theological virtues (faith, hope, and charity), which is most closely associated with prayers of petition (see CCC 2630)? Why do scriptural authors (e.g., Sir 2:8-12 and Jas 1:6-7) warn against doubt when praying for what you need?

Chapter 11

For understanding
1. **11:1-15.** In the northern campaign, what do Joshua's forces accomplish? How does Joshua win the day against an impressive coalition of troops assembled against him?
2. **11:1.** What kind of name is Jabin? What is Hazor, and where can we be certain it is located? Although Hazor is large and well-fortified, what does archaeology show about it?
3. **11:4.** How many people does a chariot hold? When is this type of advanced military technology found in Israel? What does that say about the ability of the foot soldiers of Israel?
4. **11:20.** What does the hardening of the hearts of Israel's enemies show about God? How was this mystery earlier displayed in the narrative of Exodus?
5. **11:21.** Who are the Anakim? How did sightings of the Anakim in Canaan affect Israel years earlier?

For application
1. **11:6.** The psalms often encourage readers not to be afraid even when they face overwhelming odds (e.g., Ps 91:7). Of what are you most afraid, either for yourself personally, for your family, or for anything else? How does prayer help alleviate or dissipate that fear?
2. **11:15.** How does this verse illustrate what the Holy Spirit accomplishes in the Church through apostolic succession? For example, how does apostolic succession serve to guarantee the truth of the faith you have been taught (CCC 857)?
3. **11:20.** What does Ps 95:8 mean by exhorting us not to harden our hearts? How do we harden our hearts against God? How does one recognize when his heart has actually become hardened against him?

Chapter 12

For understanding
1. **12:1–24.** Of what are these verses an inventory? How many kings did Moses dethrone east of the Jordan, and how many does Joshua oust west of the Jordan? Of what does the fact that several cities and rulers in this list are not elsewhere mentioned in the book serve as an indication?
2. **12:1.** What is the Arnon? Where is Mount Hermon? What territorial limits do both sites mark?
3. **12:7.** What does the west side of the Jordan constitute? What do scholars sometimes call it?

For application
1. **12:2.** Sihon, the Amorite king who refuses to let Israel pass peacefully through his territory but fights it instead and is conquered, is mentioned more than 30 times in the Old Testament. Why is it so important to remember the defeat of a significant enemy? Of the three enemies defeated by the Cross of Christ (the world, the flesh, and the devil), whose defeat is the most significant to you?
2. **12:2, 4.** Ps 135 and 136 celebrate the defeat of Sihon and Og as examples of God's power and his steadfast love for Israel. How has God shown his power and love in your life? What has God given you that you would not have if not for his intervention?

Chapter 13

For understanding
1. **13:1—21:45.** What do these nine chapters outline? Although some of the locations of towns and territories are no longer known with certainty today, what is the general picture of the allocation of territories to the tribes? Allegorically, according to St. Justin Martyr, how does Joshua's leading of the people into the land and giving them a temporary inheritance compare with what Jesus has accomplished?
2. **13:1.** How old was Caleb, Joshua's contemporary? Of what do the unconquered lands mainly consist? When would these regions be finally subdued?
3. **Word Study: Inheritance (13:7).** What does the Hebrew word *naḥalah* mean, and to what does it refer? What are three ways that Scripture extends this basic idea? How does the third understanding pave the way for the gospel?
4. **13:14.** Which is the one landless tribe in Israel? Instead of territory, what does it receive?

For application
1. **13:1.** Why does it seem that there is no final victory in this life, that so much remains to be done even for the old? What do you believe is your mission in life, and how much of it remains to be achieved?
2. **13:7.** What have you inherited from your family? How has this inheritance been divided or parceled out among other family members? What personal characteristics—physical, psychological, and spiritual—have you inherited, and which seem most valuable to you? What does it mean to have God as an inheritance?
3. **13:13.** Of the physical, psychological, and spiritual traits you have inherited, which represent problem areas on which you still need to work?

Chapter 14

For understanding
1. **14:1.** Who is Eleazar? What is his role in parceling out the land? Where are the sacred lots kept?
2. **14:4.** Which two tribes come from the two sons descended from Joseph in Egypt? What does their adoption into the family of Israel maintain?
3. **14:6–15.** What does Joshua grant Caleb? What are we to recall about these two men? Why does the Lord prolong Caleb's life and preserve his strength?
4. **14:10.** To what does Caleb's mention of forty-five years of prolonged life refer? What does this time span imply?

For application
1. **14:2.** How do people use lots (e.g., by drawing straws, drawing names, etc.) for decision making these days? What are some advantages of making decisions by drawing or casting lots? What are some of the disadvantages? What might be some better ways of discerning the Lord's will than by casting lots?
2. **14:8.** Caleb recalls how he maintained his trust in God even though it meant suffering the fate of those who failed to trust. Why do you think God allows such things to happen? What does it say about people like Caleb?
3. **14:14.** Caleb's fidelity was eventually rewarded. What reward can we expect by remaining faithful in a hostile world?

Chapter 15

For understanding
1. **15:1–63.** What land does the tribe of Judah inherit? What are its northern and southern borders? Why does Judah stand first in line to receive its inheritance?
2. **15:20–62.** Into what four geographical regions do the cities assigned to Judah fall?
3. **15:63.** On what border is Jerusalem situated? What do the two tribes do with the fortified settlement established there? Who finally ousts the Jebusites?

For application
1. **15:19.** If you were forced to live in an undesirable location, what might you do to improve it? How might such a circumstance be good for your character development? For example, while the desert might in many ways be an uninviting place to live, how might it be a desirable place to spend some time?

2. **15:47.** Among the cities given to Judah are places like Gaza, listed earlier in Joshua as among several of those not taken (13:2–3.). What do you know about Gaza from both biblical and even modern sources? How can a difficult place like Gaza be considered an inheritance if the inheritor is not in a position to take it? How, for example, can heaven be considered an inheritance when we have not yet taken it?

3. **15:48–60.** The "hill country" includes places with religious significance, such as Carmel (where the contest between Elijah and the priests of Baal took place). What religious association does the hill country have for Christians? How does Elizabeth address Mary when the two of them first meet (Lk 1:43)?

4. **15:63.** Jerusalem has been called the "spiritual capital of the world". What is its spiritual importance today? What is the spiritual importance of the "new Jerusalem", as the Book of Revelation describes it (Rev 21:2–3)?

Chapters 16–17

For understanding

1. **16:1—17:18.** What do these two chapters delineate? What tracts of land are acquired by these two tribes? Who has already acquired land east of the Jordan? How do these tribes rank in comparison to Judah, and why are they among the first to receive lands?

2. **16:10.** What situation does this verse confirm? What does Israel do to the surviving Canaanites who have not fallen in battle? Of what curse is this presumably the fulfillment? From whom does Genesis state that Canaan and Israel are descended?

3. **17:4.** What rule did Moses pass with regard to inheritance by daughters? What does the promise to allot land to the daughters of Zelophehad parallel?

4. **17:18.** What will deforesting parts of the hill country accomplish? How will Ephraim and Manasseh overcome the superior might of the Canaanites?

For application

1. **16:10.** Failure to eradicate evil completely in a community means that it remains to contaminate the morals of society despite efforts to control it. Can you think of any such evils that your community has failed to remove or control? What are the effects on the community? What efforts have been made to control the situation, and how successful have they been?

2. **17:4.** According to CCC 1222, the taking of the Promised Land fulfills God's covenant promise to Abraham of the land he was to inherit. Of what is this inheritance an image? How is it completely fulfilled in the New Covenant?

3. **17:14-18.** Have you ever been the executor of an estate or known someone who was? What are some of the problems that an executor faces, especially when the will is not specific or clear? What does Joshua require the tribe of Joseph to do as he tries to settle its complaint?

Chapter 18

For understanding

1. **18:1-10.** Whom does Joshua dispatch in these verses, and for what purpose? How is information about the towns and topography recorded?

2. **18:1.** In whose territory is Shiloh? Where is it with certainty located? Of what is Shiloh chosen to be the host city, and what does it become? How long does Shiloh remain in that capacity?

3. **18:11-28.** What does the tribe of Benjamin inherit? Where does the land extend horizontally? How many cities does Benjaminite territory encompass?

For application

1. **18:3.** What are some of your most important spiritual commitments (e.g., for daily prayer, Scripture study)? How often do you procrastinate about doing them? What seem to be the main excuses for doing so?

2. **18:7.** According to the word study on *inheritance* above (13:7), the Levites do not inherit land because the Lord is their inheritance. What does this mean for them? What does having the Lord as your inheritance mean for you? Why does Jesus say that it is hard for a rich man to enter the kingdom of heaven (Mt 19:23)?

3. **18:9-10.** If you and your siblings have ever had to divide an inheritance among you, what process did you follow to allocate who got what? If each person was to get equal shares, how did you determine what "equal" means? How did that process affect relationships among you? If the effects were negative (such as rifts in the family), what have you done to rectify or resolve them?

Chapters 19–20

For understanding

1. **19:1-9.** What does the tribe of Simeon inherit? How large is the tribe of Simeon, and what might be the reason for its size?

2. **19:40-48.** What does the tribe of Dan inherit? Who eventually runs it out of this territory, and where does it migrate?

3. **20:1-9.** What purpose do the six cities of refuge serve? Why is this type of protection needed? Where are the cities located? Which tribe occupies them?

4. **20:6.** What does the death of the high priest allow the innocent manslayer to do?

For application

1. **19:51.** The decisions regarding division of the land are made "before the Lord, at the door of the tent of meeting". Where do you tend to make important decisions? Why does the place matter? What difference can making an important decision before the tabernacle make?

2. **20:1-9.** Read the note for these verses. Why is it significant that the cities of refuge are occupied by Levites? Why do people go to a priest when they need help of a spiritual nature? In addition to the possible grace of a sacrament, for what are they looking?

3. **20:5.** According to CCC 1467, why does the Church require confessors to keep absolute secrecy under pain of "very severe penalties"? How does the "sacramental seal" resemble a city of refuge?
4. **20:9.** Why does Scripture command that vengeance over a crime be left to God rather than to an individual (Deut 32:35; Rom 12:19; Heb 10:30)? What does Scripture command us to do instead of exacting vengeance?

Chapter 21

For understanding
1. **21:1–42.** Where are the 48 cities that the tribe of Levi inherits? When did Moses make provision for this? How are the cities divided? Where do some lay Israelites live, and what does that mean about the clergy, practically speaking?
2. **21:43–45.** What do these verses briefly summarize? What is the major premise of Joshua's theology? What does fidelity to his pledge move Yahweh to do?
3. **21:44.** What did the initial campaigns against Canaan accomplish, and what remains to be done? What is the point about the rest referred to in this verse?

For application
1. **21:3.** According to this verse, who gave the Levites the cities in which they were to dwell? What kinds of support do the Christian people owe to their clergy (CCC 2043)?
2. **21:41–42.** Since the Levites are supported for their religious work, why is it important for them to have pasture lands? When they are not serving in a clerical capacity, how would they support themselves? How might the pasture lands have a connection with Israelite liturgical functions?
3. **21:44.** The Book of Hebrews (Heb 3:7—4:13) links the process of entering into the Lord's rest with obedience to the "living and active" word of God. How does obedience accomplish that goal? How does "hardness of heart" impede it?

Chapter 22

For understanding
1. **22:1–9.** What have the Transjordan tribes fulfilled? How does Joshua respond? How do Moses and Joshua handle their agreement to serve in the campaigns west of the Jordan?
2. **22:10–34.** What happens when the Transjordan tribes build a giant altar on the Jordan riverbank? How do the tribes west of the Jordan interpret this? How is war averted?
3. **22:17.** To what does the "sin at Peor" refer? Who remembers it well, and what is his role?
4. **22:19.** What does "the Lord's land" designate? Whose possession is the Promised Land, ultimately?

For application
1. **22:2–5.** What does Joshua tell the Transjordan tribes to do following their release from their military commitments? What is the goal of our earthly life, and how do we attain it?
2. **22:10–12.** What is rash judgment? What assumptions are the Israelites west of the Jordan making about the motives of those east of the Jordan for building the giant altar? How should we avoid the sin of judging others rashly (CCC 2477–78)?
3. **22:16–20.** Why are the Israelite delegates concerned about the suspected rebellion on the part of the Transjordan tribes? What do they fear for themselves? What do they suggest as a solution? How practical do you think the solution is for the Transjordan tribes?
4. **22:21–29.** Of what are the Transjordan tribes afraid for the future? How does that explain their conduct? How can isolation lead to distrust and even enmity among people of the same faith?

Chapter 23

For understanding
1. **23:1–16.** What is Joshua doing in these verses? With its Deuteronomic style, to what is Joshua's sermon similar?
2. **23:2.** To whom does the expression "all Israel" refer? Presumably, where does the gathering take place?
3. **23:6.** What is the "book of the law" in this instance, and where is it kept?
4. **23:7.** What is the covenant between Yahweh and Israel like? What does this mean? What will assimilation of pagan ways bring?

For application
1. **23:6–8.** How have we American Catholics in our day accommodated ourselves to the culture around us? What effects has this accommodation had on the level of faith in the Catholic Church here?
2. **23:12–13.** Why does Joshua warn against intermarriage with the Canaanites? What are some of the analogous problems that result when active Christians today intermarry with either non-practicing Christians or with unbelievers? How dire are the consequences?
3. **23:15–16.** Just as the Mosaic covenant carried blessings for obeying it and curses for violating it, what are some of the blessings and curses that attend the Christian covenant? In other words, what blessings accompany obedience to the "law of liberty", and what consequences follow from violating it (cf. Jas 1:22–25; Gal 5:13–26)?

Chapter 24

For understanding
1. **24:1–28.** What does Joshua assemble Israel at Shechem to do, and how is it similar to what happened 30 years earlier? For whom and for what purpose is this event a summons? Of what are renewal ceremonies a common feature?

Study Questions

2. **24:1.** Where in Palestine is Shechem? Where does it sit? What does the Greek LXX call this city? What might the expression "before God" indicate about the Tabernacle?
3. **24:15.** What does the covenant involve? What do the alternative choices bring?
4. **24:27.** Why is the boulder turned up on end? To what does it stand as a witness? How common is this practice of invoking witnesses in Near Eastern covenant procedures?
5. **24:29–33.** Whose deaths close out the Conquest period? Where are they buried?

For application
1. **24:14.** What (or who) are the gods that many people in our culture serve? What forms does the service of these gods take? What does it mean to "put them away"?
2. **24:15.** What does Joshua mean by his "house"? How determined are you that you and your "house" will serve the Lord? What does this determination indicate for your children or others who live with you?
3. **24:19.** Read the note for this verse. How do you understand what Joshua is saying? What does Joshua mean by saying that God is a "jealous God"? How does his "jealousy" apply to you?
4. **24:23.** What does the expression "incline your heart" mean (cf. also Ps 119:36, 112; 141:4)? How do you "incline your heart" to God?

BOOKS OF THE BIBLE

THE OLD TESTAMENT (OT)

Gen	Genesis
Ex	Exodus
Lev	Leviticus
Num	Numbers
Deut	Deuteronomy
Josh	Joshua
Judg	Judges
Ruth	Ruth
1 Sam	1 Samuel
2 Sam	2 Samuel
1 Kings	1 Kings
2 Kings	2 Kings
1 Chron	1 Chronicles
2 Chron	2 Chronicles
Ezra	Ezra
Neh	Nehemiah
Tob	Tobit
Jud	Judith
Esther	Esther
Job	Job
Ps	Psalms
Prov	Proverbs
Eccles	Ecclesiastes
Song	Song of Solomon
Wis	Wisdom
Sir	Sirach (Ecclesiasticus)
Is	Isaiah
Jer	Jeremiah
Lam	Lamentations
Bar	Baruch
Ezek	Ezekiel
Dan	Daniel
Hos	Hosea
Joel	Joel
Amos	Amos
Obad	Obadiah
Jon	Jonah
Mic	Micah
Nahum	Nahum
Hab	Habakkuk
Zeph	Zephaniah
Hag	Haggai
Zech	Zechariah
Mal	Malachi
1 Mac	1 Maccabees
2 Mac	2 Maccabees

THE NEW TESTAMENT (NT)

Mt	Matthew
Mk	Mark
Lk	Luke
Jn	John
Acts	Acts of the Apostles
Rom	Romans
1 Cor	1 Corinthians
2 Cor	2 Corinthians
Gal	Galatians
Eph	Ephesians
Phil	Philippians
Col	Colossians
1 Thess	1 Thessalonians
2 Thess	2 Thessalonians
1 Tim	1 Timothy
2 Tim	2 Timothy
Tit	Titus
Philem	Philemon
Heb	Hebrews
Jas	James
1 Pet	1 Peter
2 Pet	2 Peter
1 Jn	1 John
2 Jn	2 John
3 Jn	3 John
Jude	Jude
Rev	Revelation (Apocalypse)